HISTORICAL TOURS

WASHINGTON, DC

HELP US KEEP THIS GUIDE UP TO DATE

We would love to hear from you concerning your experiences with this guide and how you feel it could be improved and kept up to date. Please send your comments and suggestions to:

editorial@GlobePequot.com

Thanks for your input, and happy travels!

HISTORICAL TOURS

WASHINGTON, DC

Trace the Path of America's Heritage

RANDI MINETOR

Photographs by Nic Minetor

Guilford, Connecticut

An imprint of Rowman & Littlefield

Distributed by NATIONAL BOOK NETWORK

Copyright © 2015 by Rowman & Littlefield

Original base maps provided by Compass Maps, Ltd.
Updated maps © Rowman & Littlefield
Historical interior map on p. 3 courtesy of the Library of Congress.

All photographs by Nic Minetor, except for the following: Photo on p. v © Shutterstock;
photos on pp. 4, 6, 8, 9 (bottom), 10 (bottom), 11, 12 (top), 13, 25, 31, 40, 47, 52, 55,
and 65 courtesy of the Library of Congress. Plans of the Washington Monument on
p. 47 are also courtesy of the Historic American Engineering Record, National Park
Service, delineated by Paul Berry, 1986.

British Library Cataloguing in Publication Information Available

Library of Congress Cataloging-in-Publication Data Available

ISBN 978-1-4930-1273-2 (pbk.)
ISBN 978-1-4930-1779-9 (e-book)

♾™ The paper used in this publication meets the minimum requirements of American
National Standard for Information Sciences—Permanence of Paper for Printed Library
Materials, ANSI/NISO Z39.48-1992.

All the information in this guidebook is subject to change. We recommend that
you call ahead to obtain current information before traveling. All restaurants are
open daily for breakfast, lunch, and dinner, unless otherwise noted.

Contents

The National Mall's beauty intensifies at sunset.

Introduction: A Brief History of Our Nation's Capital

The war was over! After five long years of battle, the American Revolutionary War came to a triumphant end in 1781, leaving the United States of America to form its own governing body, make its own laws, and determine how, when, and where the new country would begin to take charge of its own affairs. In 1789, representatives from the thirteen states ratified the new United States Constitution—and within a year, the new country elected its first president, the victorious General George Washington, in a two-thirds majority vote of the Electoral College.

Now, the nation needed a capital, a city in which to conduct its business—and a place that would end the nomadic drift of Congress from Philadelphia to New York.

Foreseeing this need, the framers of the Constitution included a provision in the document for a "seat of government," a ten-square-mile national capital city. Congress originally chose Germantown, outside of Philadelphia, for this honor—but a decision of such magnitude tends to come with controversy, and this one was no exception. In short order, the capital's location became a bargaining chip between two of the most famous founding fathers, Thomas Jefferson of Virginia—author of the Declaration of Independence—and Alexander Hamilton of New York, the author of the Articles of Confederation.

Hamilton maintained that the federal government, not the states, should liquidate the debt the northern states accumulated during the American Revolution. Jefferson agreed with him, but wanted quid pro quo for the southern states: If the northern states were to receive this debt relief, what item of

WASHINGTON, DC	1750				1800		
	1788 Congress ratifies creation of a "seat of government of the United States."	**1790** Residency Act gives the president the power to select a site for the capital city; Thomas Jefferson and Alexander Hamilton strike a deal to place nation's capital in the southern states.	**1791** President Washington selects city site; Pierre L'Enfant creates the city's initial design.	**1792** L'Enfant is fired; Andrew Ellicott revises and publishes the design.	**1800** President John Adams moves into President's House; government moves to Washington from Philadelphia.	**1801** Congress creates Alexandria and Washington counties. Library of Congress is established.	**1802** City of Washington municipal government is created.

The Memorial to the 56 Signers of the Declaration of Independence rests in Constitution Gardens.

comparable value could the South expect? In repeated discussions in New York City, where Congress held one of many meetings to hammer out the Constitution, Jefferson and Hamilton came to an understanding: The north would get its money, and the South would get the nation's capital. Jefferson believed that the capital's proximity to the southern states would allow these states to have greater influence over the new country's financial matters.

With this negotiation point in place, the choice of the capital's exact location fell to George Washington. He selected this area along the Chesapeake

1814	1815	1824	1828	1829	1835	1846	1848
British burn the President's House, Capitol, Treasury, and other buildings; First Lady Dolley Madison saves artwork from President's House.	Thomas Jefferson sells his personal library to Congress to replace burned books.	Capitol Rotunda is completed.	Chesapeake and Ohio Canal construction begins.	James Smithson leaves $500,000 in gold to U.S. government for an institution to advance the world's knowledge.	Baltimore and Ohio Railroad arrives.	Smithsonian Institution founded.	Construction begins on Washington Monument.

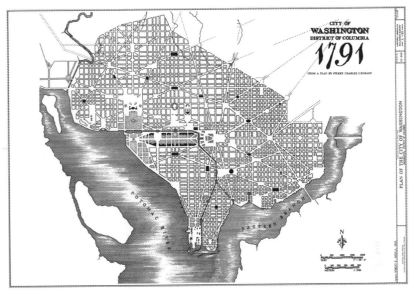

The 1791 street plan for Washington incorporated many of L'Enfant's ideas.

Bay for the many advantages it offered to the fledgling government. The land—half in Virginia and half in Maryland, at the intersection of the Potomac and Eastern Branch Rivers—provided easy access to the Atlantic Ocean and major shipping lanes, as well as a wide view of the waterways for coastal defense. Alexandria and Georgetown, two thriving neighboring cities, had already brought significant commercial activity to the area.

Now plans could move forward for the construction of the new capital city. Washington selected Andrew Ellicott, a surveyor for the new U.S. government, to determine the boundaries of the new city and the Territory of Columbia.

1850	1851	1855	1857	1859	1862	1865	1867	1871
Slave trade is abolished in Washington.	Library of Congress fire destroys nearly two-thirds of the collection.	Smithsonian Castle is completed; lack of funds halts construction of Washington Monument.	House of Representatives moves into south wing of Capitol.	Senate moves into north wing of the Capitol.	Congress abolishes slavery in Washington.	Lee surrenders to Grant at Appomattox; six days later, Lincoln is assassinated in Ford's Theatre. He dies in Petersen House the next morning.	Congress passes a law giving black men in DC the vote.	Congress abolishes the position of elected mayor of Washington, replacing it with a president-appointed governor. The territory becomes the District of Columbia.

Theodore Roosevelt renamed the President's House "The White House" in 1901.

Working with free African-American astronomer Benjamin Banneker and with his own brother, Joseph Ellicott, the surveyor laid forty boundary stones around the one hundred-square-mile territory that included the smaller capital city.

Meanwhile, Washington turned to his friend Pierre "Peter" Charles L'Enfant, a civil engineer and French-born architect who had served as General Washington's captain of engineers during the war. The passionate designer's plan included ceremonial spaces and great boulevards, creating an intersecting set of diagonal avenues over a basic grid with avenues radiat-

				1900				
1878 The DC government becomes a municipal corporation, with three commissioners appointed by the president.	**1884** Washington Monument is finally completed.	**1890** Electric lighting comes to the President's House; cable cars begin to operate in Washington.	**1897** First automobiles arrive.	**1901** McMillan Commission begins plans for redevelopment of National Mall and train station. President Teddy Roosevelt officially renames the President's House the White House.	**1907** Union Station opens on 1st Street; ground is broken for the National Cathedral.	**1910** Commission of Fine Arts is established.	**1912** The Japanese give a gift of cherry trees to America.	**1917** The U.S. enters World War I; the Mall fills with temporary buildings and war workers.

ing from the Capitol and the President's House—wide, tree-lined, and carefully placed to connect important sites throughout the city. Finally, he created fifteen circular open spaces where the avenues intersected, each a place to honor the nation's heroes with memorials and statues.

If design work had been the limit of L'Enfant's charge, his dreams might have been realized during his tenure—but he was required to work with three commissioners who would restrict the project's progress out of concern for costs and feasibility. L'Enfant, zealous to the point of obstinacy that his grand design for Washington be executed in its entirety, found himself out of a job. Washington turned L'Enfant's plan over to surveyor Andrew Ellicott, who revised it and published his version—and it was this document that became the basis for the capital city we see today.

By 1800, the President's House and Capitol Building were completed and ready for occupancy. Washington was no longer president, so John and Abigail Adams became the nation's first "first family" to live in the capital, moving in as construction of the city continued.

When the War of 1812 brought new conflict to the growing nation and its government, the British made Washington a primary target for invasion and destruction—and the Redcoats succeeded in reaching the capital city in August 1814. The President's House and the Capitol Building went up in flames on a hot August day, along with the Treasury and several other buildings in the budding capital—a moment of triumph for the British, but a temporary setback for Washington and its spirited leadership. As if in direct response to this destruction, Architect of the Capitol Benjamin Henry Latrobe would redesign these buildings in 1815, making them larger, stronger, and grander than their predecessors.

1950

1922	1924	1932	1939	1941	1943	1950–52	1953	1954
Lincoln Memorial completed.	C&O Canal ceases operation.	Supreme Court moves into its own building.	Daughters of the American Revolution turn away African-American singer Marian Anderson, who is scheduled to sing at Constitution Hall. First Lady Eleanor Roosevelt arranges for Anderson to sing on the steps of the Lincoln Memorial for 75,000 people.	The Japanese attack Pearl Harbor, and the U.S. enters the War in the Pacific.	Pentagon construction is completed.	Massive renovation of the White House.	The Supreme Court ends segregation in Washington's restaurants.	The Supreme Court rules that school segregation is unlawful; Washington integrates its schools.

Capitol building after the fire, August 24, 1814.

President John Madison signed the Treaty of Ghent in 1815 in the Octagon, just a block from the site of the President's House reconstruction, and a new spirit of progress gripped the nation's capital. The population expanded with the increase of opportunities, and an influx of free African-Americans became business owners and skilled craftsmen . . . while agricultural estates with slaves ringed the city's outskirts. By the mid-1830s, when Washington's population broke 20,000, the conflict between states' rights and abolition made the city a hotbed of racial struggle, with clashes between slave owners, free blacks, and abolitionists becoming regular events on the capital's streets.

When the Civil War started, President Abraham Lincoln moved as quickly as he could to bring freedom to Washington's slaves, convincing Congress to abolish slavery in the federal district on April 16, 1862. By the end of the war, with President Andrew Johnson in charge after Lincoln's assassination—just days after Confederate General Robert E. Lee's surrender to the Union at Appomattox—all slaves were free throughout the reunited states. Washington officials moved quickly to create the Freedmen's Bureau, to provide freed African-Americans with food, housing jobs, and education.

1961	1962	1963	1965	1967	1968	1970	1971	1972
23rd Amendment gives Washington residents the vote for president.	Streetcar service ends in Washington after 99 years.	Martin Luther King Jr. delivers his "I Have a Dream" speech to an audience of 200,000.	Capital Beltway opens.	President Johnson appoints Walter E. Washington as the mayor of Washington, DC	The assassination of Martin Luther King in Memphis leads to rioting and deaths in Washington.	DC gets a delegate (non-voting) in the House of Representatives.	Kennedy Center for the Performing Arts opens.	A break-in at Democratic National Headquarters in the Watergate office complex leads to an investigation. China gives two pandas to the National Zoo.

In the late 1800s, with its population swelling with job seekers on a daily basis and a ring of slums surrounding the Capitol district, Congress recognized the need to end decades of neglect and rescue the capital city from implosion.

Enter the McMillan Commission

In 1901, Congress formed the Senate Park Improvement Commission of the District of Columbia, headed by Senator James McMillan of Michigan. Inspired by L'Enfant's plan and by the great capitals of European countries, the commission developed a plan to replace the old, dilapidated, and shoddy construction in Washington with deliberately artful government buildings, parks, and monuments. The massive reconstruction was underway by 1902 and continued until 1922, with an interruption of several years during World War I—reaching its completion with the dedication of the Lincoln Memorial on May 30, 1922. The beautified city received another round of concentrated labor in the 1930s, when President Franklin Roosevelt's Works Progress Administration put thousands of people to work in Washington and gave the city the next level of required polishing.

Long Overdue Changes

With no voice in Congress and antiquated laws stating that they could not even vote for president, the people of the District of Columbia stood as the most underrepresented citizens of the United States. This changed in 1967, when President Lyndon Johnson removed the three-commissioner system of

1974	1976	1979	1981	1984	1987	1988	1990	1993	1995
President Richard Nixon resigns.	America's bicentennial draws more than a million people to the National Mall.	Pope John Paul II says mass on the National Mall.	President Ronald Reagan is shot outside the Washington Hilton; he recovers.	Renovation of the Old Post Office completed.	Smithsonian Quadrangle opens.	Renovation of Union Station creates a major shopping and dining complex.	Washington National Cathedral is finally completed.	Holocaust Memorial Museum opens.	Korean War Veterans Memorial opens.
	Washington Metro Subway opens.								
	National Air and Space Museum opens.								

World War I troops parade down Pennsylvania Avenue.

government and instated a mayor, a city council, and a planned election of a
Congressional delegate in 1971.

Today's Washington continues to grow and change. New memorials have
been added on the National Mall, commemorating World War II, Korean War
veterans, and, most recently, Dr. Martin Luther King Jr. Ford's Theatre has
undergone a significant renovation that includes a new museum focused on
the assassination of Abraham Lincoln, and an extensive visitor center for the
Capitol Building improves the visitor experience with interpretive displays
and interactive materials. Every year, Washington attracts new residents and
millions of visitors with its ability to match the drama of history with its blend
of culture, art, historic preservation, and rich international diversity.

2000

1997	1998	1999	2001	2004	2011	2012	2014
Franklin Delano Roosevelt Memorial opens.	Ronald Reagan International Trade Center opens. Federal Triangle is finally completed.	African-American Civil War Memorial opens.	A terrorist attack on September 11 destroys part of the Pentagon, killing 125 people.	National World War II Memorial opens.	Martin Luther King Jr. Memorial opens.	Lincoln Memorial reflecting pool restoration completed.	Washington Monument reopens after extensive restoration.

Key Figures in Washington's History

Mary McLeod Bethune Founder of Bethune-Cookman University in Daytona Beach, Bethune came to Washington to charter the National Council of Negro Women. She rose to prominence as the first black woman to hold a leadership position on the federal level, heading the Division of Negro Affairs of the National Youth Administration and becoming an important member of Franklin Roosevelt's Black Cabinet.

Mary McLeod Bethune lived in the Council House during her tenure as its president.

John Wilkes Booth On April 14, 1865, this actor and Southern extremist assassinated President Abraham Lincoln in Ford's Theatre with a gunshot to the back of the president's head. Booth broke his leg during his getaway, but managed to mount a horse and ride off into Virginia, where the 16th New York Cavalry Regiment caught up with him on April 26. In the ensuing skirmish, Booth took a bullet in the neck and died three hours later.

The actor John Wilkes Booth.

Alexander Hamilton The author of the Articles of Confederation, the precursor to the U.S. Constitution, Hamilton represented the North's interests in the discussion of the capital city's location. He traded the capital for debt relief of the northern states' war expenditures, paving the way for a capital city in the southern United States.

The Thomas Jefferson Memorial is one of the most popular stops in Washington.

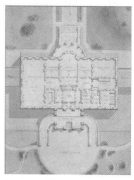

Latrobe's 1807 site plan for the President's House.

Thomas Jefferson Before he became America's third president, Jefferson was one of three commissioners chosen to supervise the construction of Washington. It was his negotiation with fellow framer Alexander Hamilton that led to the selection of this triangle of land on the Potomac River as the ideal location for the capital.

Jacqueline Kennedy The wife of our thirty-fifth president, Jacqueline Kennedy redecorated the White House with the goal of bringing each room a sense of history, scouring government warehouses for pieces that once stood in the White House and asking the nation to donate items of historical significance. Her efforts turned the house into a model of historic preservation, and the position of White House Curator was created to prevent the collection from ever being dismantled. The first lady went on to invite the nation's most prominent performing artists to the White House, bringing opera, ballet, jazz, and classical theater to the president's home—and her work to establish a national cultural center in Washington eventually blossomed into the John F. Kennedy Center for the Performing Arts, which was dedicated in 1971.

Benjamin Henry Latrobe The British-born architect of the Capitol Building, Latrobe went on to design Decatur House and St. John's Episcopal Church. After the British burned the capital city in 1814, Latrobe took charge of the reconstruction, redesigning the interior of the Capitol Building and adding porticos to the President's House. It's his design that we continue to admire today.

Pierre Charles L'Enfant A civil engineer and French-born architect, L'Enfant served as General Washington's captain of engineers during the American Revolutionary War. Washington entrusted him with the grand design for the capital city, a responsibility L'Enfant took so seriously that he refused any deviation from his original design to save money or time. He was fired and never received any payment from the government, but his city plan finally came to fruition in the early twentieth century.

Abraham Lincoln The sixteenth American president and the commander in chief throughout the American Civil War, Lincoln worked to abolish slavery in Washington first, ahead of the rest of the nation, and succeeded in 1862. Among his many accomplishments was the delivery of the Emancipation Proclamation in 1863, abolishing slavery in the Confederate states.

Abraham Lincoln, photographed by Alexander Gardner.

Dolley Madison The wife of our fourth president, James Madison, was well known as a spirited patriot in her own right. As first lady when it was clear that the British were about to invade the capital, she had the foresight to insist that many works of art in the President's House be removed and placed in hiding. The British arrived and burned down the President's House, but Gilbert Stuart's famous portrait of George Washington was saved from the inferno.

Mathew Brady's photo of Dolley Madison in 1848.

James McMillan

Andrew W. Mellon

James McMillan In 1901, this Michigan senator took on the redevelopment of a plan to transform Washington into a beautiful city with classic architecture, green spaces, monuments and memorials, and the sense of grandeur associated with the most prominent European capitals. Reexamining the L'Enfant design and working with some of the era's top architects and advisors, the McMillan Commission called for creation of the National Mall and a major railway station for the capital city. After twenty years of reconstruction, Washington became the city we see today.

Andrew W. Mellon This brilliant financier from Pittsburgh made his fortune in banking, oil, shipbuilding, steel, and investments in aluminum, silicon carbide (an industrial abrasive), and processes for turning industrial waste into usable material, giving him the discretionary income to amass an extraordinary collection of art from all over the world. He bequeathed his collection to the United States for creation of the National Gallery of Art, along with $10 million for the museum's construction.

President Franklin Roosevelt was re-elected three times, before Congress set a term limit for the presidency.

Franklin Delano Roosevelt The thirty-second president of the United States promised America a New Deal that would end the Great Depression, putting citizens to work on projects that strengthened infrastructure and beautified cities. Washington was one of the major beneficiaries of the Works Progress Administration, receiving a citywide face-lift with new roads, bridges, utility systems, gardens and parklands, and employing thousands of workers who would have suffered in poverty without the work this program provided.

Alexander Robey Shepherd Governor of Washington, DC, in the 1870s, Shepherd began a modernization of the city that included paving the roads, building a covered sewer system, and bringing utilities into the capital. His tenure was short-lived, however, as Congress determined that his spending was out of control. As a result, Congress dissolved the position of governor and reinstated the three-commissioner system, taking back control of Washington.

James Smithson For reasons that remain unclear even today, this well-invested British mineralogist chose to leave his entire fortune—more than $500,000—to the United States for the establishment of an institution "for the increase and diffusion of knowledge." His bequest became the foundation for creation of the Smithsonian Institution.

Mary Church Terrell At eighty-six years old, Terrell took on the antiquated Washington laws that restricted black citizens from being served in white restaurants. Her three-year crusade ended when the U.S. Supreme Court took her part, abolishing segregation in the city's restaurants in 1953.

George Washington Our nation's first president set the wheels in motion for a capital city of which the country could be proud. He chose Pierre L'Enfant as the original designer of the new city that would bear the president's name, completed the land purchase on behalf of the government, and approved construction of the new city.

President Washington and his family.

Tour 1: Pre-1800–1850

Washington: The End of the Manors, the Beginning of a Nation

Washington, DC

In 1790, when George Washington chose this diamond-shaped slice of land to become the site of the nation's capital, this territory was divided into a network of manor houses and estates, farmed by slaves. Here at the intersection of the Potomac and Eastern Branch Rivers, colonists were attracted to the farthest point to which large ships could navigate up the Potomac. There they established an early settlement, formalizing it as Georgetown in 1751. The new town quickly became an inland center of trade and commerce.

Once construction of the nation's capital city began, residents recognized the arrival of a period of considerable change throughout this corner of Maryland and Virginia. Landowners with large estates objected strongly to the purchase of their land for creation of a city, finally agreeing to an arrangement through which they would keep half their land, while the government would pay a fair price for the rest. Washington brought Pierre L'Enfant to the table to begin the grand plan for the majestic capital city, while Andrew Ellicott and Benjamin Banneker set up the forty sandstone markers that delineated the boundaries of the capital district.

Despite the urgent need for a capital city, the fledgling capital did not receive adequate financial support from Congress to grow and flourish from the outset. L'Enfant was forced to abandon his

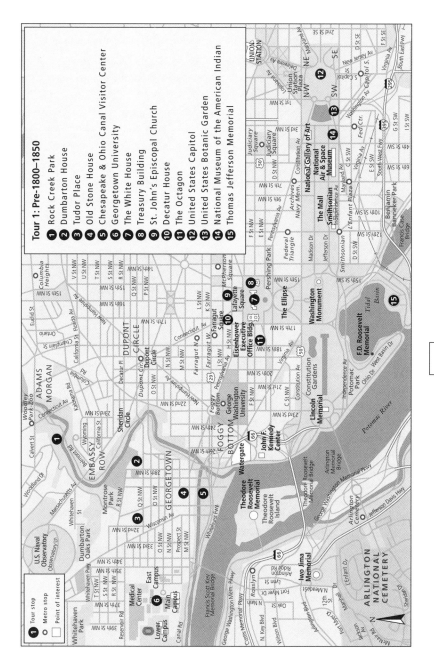

Tour 1: Pre-1800–1850

1. Rock Creek Park
2. Dumbarton House
3. Tudor Place
4. Old Stone House
5. Chesapeake & Ohio Canal Visitor Center
6. Georgetown University
7. The White House
8. Treasury Building
9. St. John's Episcopal Church
10. Decatur House
11. The Octagon
12. United States Capitol
13. United States Botanic Garden
14. National Museum of the American Indian
15. Thomas Jefferson Memorial

How to Find the Four Original Cornerstones

To the south: The marker is at Jones Point Lighthouse in Alexandria—in an opening in the seawall, where the stone was hidden until 1912.

To the west: Andrew Ellicott Park at 2824 N. Arizona Street, south of West Street in Falls Church, Virginia, has the second marker.

To the north: The marker resides at the west corner of Arlington County, at the 1880 block of the East-West Highway in Silver Spring, Maryland, just south of the highway at the edge of a forest.

To the east: Find the marker between Seat Pleasant and Capitol Heights, about 100 feet east of the intersection of Eastern and Southern Avenues.

There's more information on the locations of all forty boundary stones at www.boundarystones.org.

One wing of the Capitol only had been erected, which with the President's House, a mile distant, both constructed with white sandstone, were shining objects in dismal contrast with the scene around them. Instead of recognizing the avenues and streets portrayed in the plan of the city, not one was visible, unless we except a road with two buildings on each side of it called the New Jersey Avenue. The Pennsylvania Avenue, leading as laid down on paper, from the Capitol to the President's Mansion, was then nearly the whole distance a deep morass, covered with alder bushes. . . . The roads in every direction were muddy and unimproved. . . . In short, it was a 'new settlement.'

John Cotton Smith, member of Congress from Connecticut in the Sixth Congress

project just ten months after he began it, when he met resistance to completing the entire design from the commissioners—Thomas Jefferson, Daniel Carroll, and David Stuart. By the time the President's House and Capitol Building were ready for occupancy in 1800, only a fraction of L'Enfant's grand plan was in place, the rest of it either under construction or shelved until additional funds could be acquired.

Meanwhile, rumblings of another war began to increase in volume as the nineteenth century began. The War of 1812 gained momentum until the English navy succeeded in reaching the capital city in August 1814, and while First Lady Dolley Madison quickly thought to rescue the artwork, members of Congress secured the Declaration of Independence and the Constitution, keeping them safe while the British set fire to the city. In one day, on August 24, the British burned the War Department, the Treasury Building, the President's House, and the Capitol—and they would have left nothing but charred remains, had it not been for a driving rain that fell that night, drenching the burning buildings and quenching the fire.

As reconstruction began, workmen had no choice but to paint the burnt-black President's House with white paint, changing its appearance so completely that area residents began to call it the "White House." (President Theodore Roosevelt would officially rename the building the White House in 1901.)

With the war ended and a new sense of optimism bubbling throughout the country, Washington's development could move forward again. Construction began on the Chesapeake and Ohio Canal, which would bring raw goods and products from the nation's interior states to the capital, cementing Washington's place as a national port and commercial center. As the canal neared its final length, however, the Baltimore and Ohio Railroad arrived in Washington, opening the city to an unprecedented level of commercial activity—and signaling the slower canal route's imminent decline.

Begin your tour of Washington's earliest days in Georgetown, where many historic sites hearken back to the late 1700s and early 1800s. You'll find a fascinating contrast between wealthy, genteel landowners' lives and the simple home of a local carpenter, as well as the beginnings of commercial activity that would grow to place Washington at the heart of international trade, making the city a conduit to the nation's interior states and a hub of daily market activity.

The sky was brilliantly illuminated by the different conflagrations, and a dark red light was thrown upon the road, sufficient to permit each man to view distinctly his comrade's face. . . . When the detachment sent out to destroy Mr. Madison's house entered his dining parlor, they found a dinner table spread and covers laid for forty guests. . . . They sat down to it, . . . and, having satisfied their appetites with fewer complaints than would have probably escaped their rival gourmands, and partaken pretty freely of the wines, they finished by setting fire to the house which had so liberally entertained them. **George Robert Gleig, a British soldier who participated in the attack on Washington, August 24, 1814**

Start your tour at Rock Creek Park, on the eastern edge of Georgetown. Peirce Mill is found at the corner of Tilden Street NW (Park Road) and Beach Drive.

1. Rock Creek Park, including Peirce Mill. Here you can view the local terrain as it may have appeared before European settlers set foot on the land. Prehistoric deposits in this park match the Late Woodland period, 500 BC to 1600 AD, when the first human beings populated this area—and radiocarbon dating proves that deposits along the river date back to the last Ice Age. Artifacts tell us that native people from many areas congregated here, below Great Falls, to live, trade, and fish. Stop at Peirce Mill, the last of its kind from the days when farmers used the creek's power to grind meal and flour in the late eighteenth century. Follow Rock Creek Parkway north to Beach Drive, north of the National Zoo, where this national park

Peirce Mill is the last mill of its kind in Washington.

begins. (202) 895-6070, www.nps.gov/rocr. Always open. Free. Metro: Friendship Heights (for the Nature Center). GEORGETOWN.

2. Dumbarton House. Among this 1804 house's many distinguished guests was First Lady Dolley Madison, who stayed here briefly when she fled the President's House during the British invasion in 1814. Now owned by the National Society of the Colonial Dames of America, Dumbarton House underwent an extensive renovation in 1991 to return it to its original Adamesque style and nineteenth-century character. Visitors enjoy touring the beautifully appointed rooms and seeing the furniture, paintings, and household items used by the wealthy and well-bred in the early days of the nation's capital city. 2715 Q Street NW, (202) 337-2288, www.dumbartonhouse.org. Tours T–Su 11–3; closed federal holidays. Adults $5, children and students with ID free. Metro: Dupont Circle. GEORGETOWN.

3. Tudor Place. One family, led by Thomas and Martha Custis Peter, owned this home for nearly 200 years, and this grand residence features elements left behind by many generations. Martha, granddaughter of George Washington, received many items from Mount Vernon that are displayed here, including gilded brackets in the salon and Washington's own camp chair in the parlor. Don't miss Francis Scott Key's desk, the stunning Belgian chandelier in the drawing room—where the Peters once entertained General Lafayette, Washington's aide-de-camp—and the manual typewriters and early 1900s telephones in the study. 1644 31st Street NW, (202) 965-0400, www.tudorplace.org.

Our kind friend, Mr. Carroll, has come to hasten my departure, and is in a very bad humour with me because I insist on waiting until the large picture of General Washington is secured, and it requires to be unscrewed from the wall . . .

And now, dear sister, I must leave this house, or the retreating army will make me a prisoner in it by filling up the road I am directed to take.

Dolley Madison's letter to her sister Lucy Payne Washington Todd, August 24, 1814

There is about the whole place an air of dignity and unity of design seen in no other of the old place in the District.

Records of the Columbia Historical Society, Washington, DC, 1915

George Washington's grand-daughter lived at Tudor Place.

Tours T–Sa 10–4, Su 12–4; closed January and federal holidays. Adults $10, seniors (62+) and military $8, students 5–17 $3, children under 5 free (tour not recommended for young children). Metro: Dupont Circle or Foggy Bottom. GEORGETOWN.

4. Old Stone House. The oldest standing building in the District of Columbia, this little home was built in 1765 by Christopher Layman, a cabinetmaker who used it as a residence and shop. With all of the grandeur associated with a national capital, it's

A common merchant lived in the Old Stone House, in a very different style from rich Washingtonians.

good to have this opportunity to see how the common citizens lived. 3051 M Street, (202) 895-6070, www.nps.gov/olst. W–Su 12–5; closed New Year's Day, July 4, Thanksgiving, Christmas. Free. Metro: Foggy Bottom. GEORGETOWN.

5. Chesapeake and Ohio Canal National Historical Park. Take a boat tour of the canal on a barge pulled from the towpath by mules, and enjoy the same leisurely pace that nineteenth-century merchants experienced as they brought their goods to market. Since 1830, the first section of the 184.5-mile canal served as the main artery for the transport of coal, lumber, grain, and other agricultural products, with the route to Cumberland, Maryland, finally opening in 1850. In winter, when the boat ride is not running, the bookstore and visitor center remain open. 1057 Thomas Jefferson Street NW, (202) 653-5190, www.nps.gov/choh. Apr–Oct, daily 9–4:45, weekends in late fall and

See the original locks on the Chesapeake & Ohio Canal.

Archbishop John Carroll founded Georgetown University.

I've had the second floor where we live examined — and it is about to fall down! The engineer said that the ceiling in the state dining room only stayed up from force of habit!
From a letter President Harry S Truman wrote to his sister Mary Jane Truman, 1948

early spring, 9–4:45. Boat ride $5. Metro: Foggy Bottom. GEORGETOWN.

6. Georgetown University. Founded in 1789 by Archbishop John Carroll, Georgetown is the oldest Catholic and Jesuit university in the United States. A walk around this campus reveals classic archi-tecture alongside modern construction, with the grand White-Gravenor Hall (housing administra-tive offices and the College of Arts & Sciences) and Healy and Copley Halls representing the traditionally ornate gothic styles. Prospect and 35th Streets to 27th and O Streets NW, (202) 687-0100, www .georgetown.edu. Campus always open for self-guided tours. Free. Metro: Rosslyn or Dupont Circle. GEORGETOWN.

There are no Metrorail stops in Georgetown. From the university, take the Metrobus Orange Line and continue your tour at the White House.

7. The White House. The exterior stone walls you see today stood here in 1800, on the day that President John Adams and First Lady Abigail Adams moved into the President's House. Since then, every U.S. president has lived here, although James and Dolley Madison were forced to room elsewhere after the British torched the house in 1814, and another fire, during Herbert Hoover's presidency, led to a short evacuation.

Today, after an extensive renovation ordered by Harry and Bess Truman, the White House has 132 rooms on six levels, including thirty-five bathrooms and twenty-eight fireplaces. To get a tour ticket, arrive before 7:30 a.m. at the Visitor Center — and get in line much earlier during the busy spring and

summer seasons. (On a snowy winter day, you may have the tour to yourself.) The newly renovated White House Visitor Center has interactive multimedia exhibits for viewing before your tour, to enrich your tour experience. 1600 Pennsylvania Avenue; Visitor Center is at 1450 Pennsylvania Avenue NW, (202) 208-1631, www.nps.gov/whho.

Tours T–Th 7:30–11 a.m., F 7:30 a.m.–12 p.m., Sa 7:30 a.m.–1 p.m., closed Su. Visitor Center daily 7:30–4; closed Thanksgiving, Christmas, New Year's Day. Free. Metro: Federal Triangle or Metro Center. DOWNTOWN.

8. Treasury Building. The oldest department building in Washington, this classical 1842 edifice houses the offices of the Department of the Treasury—*not* the production of United States currency (that's the Bureau of Engraving; see page 45). On the tour, you'll see the suite of offices used by Treasury Secretary Salmon P. Chase during the Civil War, the secretary's conference room and

Today's White House features Latrobe's stunning porticos.

diplomatic reception room, and the rooms used by President Andrew Johnson as a temporary White House in the days after Lincoln's assassination. Most interesting is the Burglar-Proof Vault, an iron wall built in 1864 to prevent unwanted plundering of the nation's funds. 1500 Pennsylvania Avenue NW, (202) 622-2000, www.treas.gov. Tours Saturday morning by reservation only; contact your congressional representative's office for available dates and tickets. Free.

9. St. John's Episcopal Church. Every president since James Madison has attended services here at the "Church of the Presidents." This neighborhood church was designed by the official Architect of the Capitol, Benjamin Henry Latrobe, who also redesigned the Capitol Building and the President's House after the 1814 fires. While Latrobe supervised the reconstruction of those two structures, he found time to create this simple, elegant, neoclassical house of worship—and to compose a hymn that he played on the organ at the first service held here in 1816. Later renovations expanded the building and its seating, and added stained glass, marble, and a modern lighting system. 1525 H St NW at Lafayette Square, (202) 347-8766, www.stjohns-dc. org. Visitors are welcome to join the parish for worship on Sundays; check the website for schedule. Free. Metro: McPherson Square. DOWNTOWN.

10. Decatur House. The first private residence constructed on Lafayette Square, this home was the fourth project by Benjamin Henry Latrobe, who also designed the Capitol, the President's House, and nearby St. John's Episcopal Church. Commodore Stephen Decatur of the U.S. Navy and his

The "Church of the Presidents" nestles between tall modern buildings a few blocks from the White House.

wife lived here for fourteen months before Decatur's untimely death—he was the loser of a gentlemen's duel with Commodore James Barron over some remarks Decatur had made about Barron's performance in battle. Decatur's widow, Susan, rented the house to a long list of luminaries including three secretaries of state: Henry Clay, Martin Van Buren, and Edward Livingston. In 1956, a bequest left the house to the National Trust for Historic Preservation. 1610 H Street NW at Jackson Place, www.decaturhouse.org. Tours Mondays only at 11, 12:30, and 2. Closed on Monday holidays. Free. Metro: Farragut West and Farragut North. DOWNTOWN.

The old house has opened its doors to nearly every President from Madison down, and to all the greatest men and most beautiful women of America and Europe for a hundred years.
From *Historic Houses of Washington* by Teunis S. Hamlin, 1893

11. The Octagon. Built from 1799 to 1801 for Colonel John Tayloe III, a rich Virginia plantation owner, the Octagon (which is actually six-sided)

The Octagon actually has six sides.

When the news of peace arrived we all went crazy with joy. Miss Sally Coles, a cousin of Mrs. Madison, from the head of the stairs cried out "Peace! Peace!" and told the butler, John Freeman, to serve out without stint wine to all within. I played the President's March on the violin.

President Madison's valet, working at The Octagon in 1814, recounting the reaction in the house when news of peace with England was announced

I am not one of those who can sneer at the Capitol. Its faults, like the faults of a friend are sacred. I know them, but wish to name them not, save to the one who only can remedy . . . The surface blemish vexes, the pretentious splendor offends. These are not the Capitol. We look deeper, we look higher, to find beauty, to see sublimity, to see the Capitol, august and imperishable!

Mary Clemmer, *Ten Years in Washington*, 1882

became the two-year home of President and Dolley Madison after the burning of the President's House. On February 17, 1815, in the home's second-floor parlor, Madison signed the Treaty of Ghent to end the War of 1812. The American Institute of Architects purchased the building from the Tayloes in 1902, completing several restorations before selling it to the American Architectural Foundation, which opened it to the public. 1799 New York Avenue, (202) 626-7439, http://www .nps.gov/nr/travel/wash/dc22.htm. Th–Sa 1–4, free. Metro: Farragut West and Farragut North. DOWNTOWN.

From the Octagon, walk east on E Street between the White House and the Ellipse, and continue past Freedom Plaza to Pennsylvania Avenue. Bear right on Pennsylvania and walk to the Capitol Building. If you prefer, take the Metrobus Red or Green Line down Pennsylvania to the Capitol Visitor Center.

12. United States Capitol. On a site chosen by L'Enfant for its slight elevation and view of the city, the Capitol Building opened to Congress on November 17, 1800, with just one wing in operation—and while three more wood-frame wings were constructed over the next thirteen years, they burned to the ground in 1814, and were not replaced until later in the nineteenth century. Today, we can enjoy the dome and rotunda added in the 1860s, with the spectacular painting by Constantino Brumidi on the inside of the dome. The 580,000-foot, three-level Capitol Visitor Center, which opened December 2, 2008, now serves as the main point of entry—you'll find a street-level entrance to the underground center on the east side of the Capitol building. Stop here to book your tour of the Capitol, visit the Exhibition Hall, get a bite to eat in the restaurant, or admire the Capitol dome through the center's six skylights. East Capitol and 1st Streets NE, (202) 226-8000, www.visitthecapitol.gov. M–Sa 8:30–4:30; closed Sunday, Thanksgiving, Christmas, New Year's Day, Inauguration Day. Free. Metro: Union Station, Capitol South, or Federal Center SW. DOWNTOWN.

13. United States Botanic Garden. The oldest continually operating botanic garden in the country was conceived in 1842, when naval officer Charles Wilkes returned from circumnavigating the globe in the United States Exploring Expedition to the South Seas. Wilkes brought back a huge collection of totally unfamiliar live and dried plants, but the government had no appropriate space in which to store and study these hard-won specimens. With no better alternative, they were housed in a specially constructed greenhouse in the Old Patent Office until the original Botanic Garden—built where the Capitol's reflecting pool is now—reached completion. Today, four plants in the garden are either actual plants collected by Wilkes or descendants of his specimens. The entire Botanic Garden moved to its current location in 1933; the building was transformed again by an extensive renovation from 1997 to 2001. Capitol Building grounds, 100 Maryland Avenue SW, (202) 225-8333, www.usbg.gov. Daily 10–5. Free. Metro: Federal Center SW or Capitol South. DOWNTOWN.

Be sure to stop at the visitor center at the Capitol Building.

Historical Tours

14. National Museum of the American Indian.
Completed in 2004, this addition to the Smithsonian is the first national museum dedicated to the Native American perspective and experience—not just as a part of history, but as a living culture in today's America. Welcome screens at the entrance greet visitors in 150 Native languages, and six permanent exhibitions display 8,000 objects from the museum's collection in galleries themed around the history, spirituality, and contemporary lives of the continent's indigenous people. Return to a Native Place: Algonquian Peoples of the Chesapeake tells the story of the people who lived in this region before Europeans arrived. 4th Street and Independence Avenue SW, (202) 633-1000, www.nmai.si.edu. Daily 10–5:30; closed Christmas. Free. Metro: Smithsonian. NATIONAL MALL.

To complete your tour, take the Metrobus Green Line or Red Line from the Capitol to the Jefferson Memorial on the Tidal Basin.

15. Thomas Jefferson Memorial. We know him best for writing the Declaration of Independence, but our third president's influence extended far beyond parchment and quill. President Thomas Jefferson completed the Louisiana Purchase, more than doubling the nation's geographic size overnight, and he ordered and sponsored the Lewis and Clark expedition, a scientific exploration that broadened and deepened the country's understanding of the continent's natural wonders. Designed to reflect Jefferson's own sensibilities as an architect, this monument is reminiscent of the Pantheon in Rome, echoing the ancient

A letter from you calls up recollections very dear to my mind. It carries me back to the times when, beset with difficulties and dangers, we were fellow-laborers in the same cause, struggling for what is most valuable to man, his right of self-government. Laboring always at the same oar, with some wave ever a head, threatening to overwhelm us, and yet passing harmless under our bark, we knew not how we rode through the storm with heart and hand, and made a happy port. Still, we did not expect to be without rubs and difficulties; and we have had them.

Thomas Jefferson writing to John Adams, Monticello, January 21, 1812

Washington, DC

Who Is This Man, and Why Does He Get a Memorial?

You'll see him sitting near the Tidal Basin within his own pergola, in East Potomac Park on the southeast side of East Basin Drive—just before the Inlet Bridge to the Franklin Roosevelt Memorial. Life-size, in his waistcoat with his hair carefully curled, George Mason looks serene in cast bronze, as if taking pleasure in the landscape before him. Mason wrote the Virginia Declaration of Rights, the document that became the basis for the Bill of Rights and for portions of the Declaration of Independence. He insisted that an explicit statement of personal rights be added to the Constitution—and when his fellow congressmen did not initially add the bill, Mason refused to sign. Eventually, he convinced them to add the first ten amendments to the Constitution. It's Mason to whom we owe our freedom of speech, religion, peaceful assembly, and the press, our right to bear arms, and to the due process of law. The George Mason Memorial commemorates the man who articulated these fundamental issues.

End your day at the Tidal Basin, when the Jefferson Memorial looks its best.

circular structure and incorporating elements of the classic style with which Jefferson identified. It's a fitting tribute to one of the most brilliant men in U.S. history, and a peaceful, comfortable place to end the day's tour. On the Tidal Basin, (202) 426-6841, www.nps.gov/thje. Open 24 hours year-round. Free. Metro: Smithsonian or L'Enfant Plaza. NATIONAL MALL.

Whenever it is proposed to prepare plans for the Capitol, I should prefer the adoption of some one of the models of antiquity which have had the approbation of thousands of years; and for the President's house I should prefer the celebrated fronts of modern buildings which have already received the approbation of all good judges.

From Thomas Jefferson's letter to Pierre L'Enfant, April 10, 1791

Tour 2: 1851–1900

The Nation Develops, Splits, and Reunites

As the Northern call for abolition intensified, Washington became a flashpoint for racial tension and unrest. People from every side of the slavery issue lived and worked in the capital city: Free blacks, slaves, white slave owners, and passionate abolitionists faced one another in the streets, in public houses, and in places of business.

Slave pens—where slave owners deposited their property until the slaves were sold at auction—sprang up around Lafayette Square in full view of the President's House, receiving notices

Slave pens sprang up within sight of the President's House.

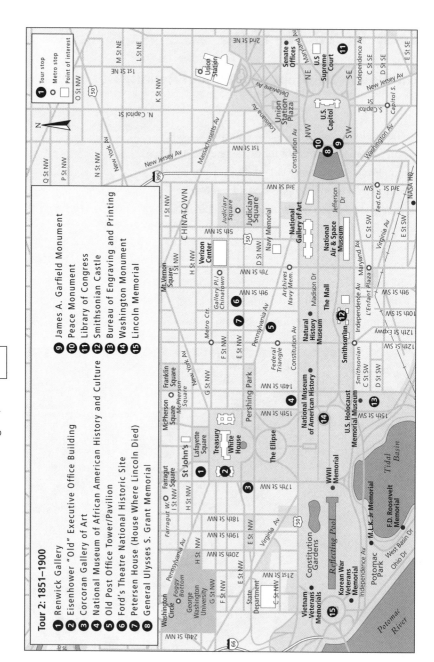

Tour 2: 1851–1900

1. Renwick Gallery
2. Eisenhower "Old" Executive Office Building
3. Corcoran Gallery of Art
4. National Museum of African American History and Culture
5. Old Post Office Tower/Pavilion
6. Ford's Theatre National Historic Site
7. Petersen House (House Where Lincoln Died)
8. General Ulysses S. Grant Memorial
9. James A. Garfield Monument
10. Peace Monument
11. Library of Congress
12. Smithsonian Castle
13. Bureau of Engraving and Printing
14. Washington Monument
15. Lincoln Memorial

Legend:
- 1 Tour stop
- o Metro stop
- □ Point of interest

of disgust in newspapers as far away as Boston. In 1848, seventy-seven slaves attempted a daring escape from Washington aboard a ship called the *Pearl,* sailing in the dead of night toward freedom in Pennsylvania. Bad weather forced them to drop anchor, however, making them easy targets for recapture—and they were returned to Washington for sale to plantations.

As the government expanded to manage the coming war, Washington's population swelled as well—and with more people on the city's streets, conflicts between Northern and Southern sympathizers escalated. Raids and fights in the streets became almost commonplace.

In 1861, as shots were fired at Fort Sumter and the war began in earnest, President Lincoln put an innovative program in place in the District of Columbia: He encouraged Congress to pass the District of Columbia Emancipation Act, in which the government offered payment to slave owners in exchange for their slaves' freedom. Congress obliged and turned the act into law on April 16, 1862, abolishing slavery in the District many months before the South was forced to do the same. This was the only program of its kind in the United States, and it had the desired effect: Slave owners responded and traded human beings for cash, considering this a relatively fair deal.

With war came the construction of a circle of forts around the District of Columbia, to protect the capital from another invading force and potential disaster. Only one of these forts ever saw combat: On July 12, 1864, Fort Stevens became the center of a sortie between General Jubal Early's Confederate forces and the Union's VI Corps—by

It weighted anchor at two o'clock that night, carrying with it these persons, of whom thirty-eight were men, twenty-six women, and thirteen male children. Soon after daybreak, when the flight was discovered, a small steamer containing thirty armed men was sent in pursuit of the schooner. Quite a distance down the river she was sighted, captured without resistance, and the vessel and crew brought to Washington. The slaves were returned to their owners, and the men in command . . . were convicted and sentenced to a long term of confinement in the city jail.
Records of the Columbia Historical Society, Washington, DC, 1900

Fort Washington is one of many Third System forts in the District.

Here . . . is the place where President Lincoln stood, witnessing the fight; there, by his side, a surgeon was wounded by a minie ball. I entreated the President not to expose his life to the bullets of the enemy; but he seemed oblivious to his surroundings; finally, . . . I said, "Mr. President, I know you are commander of the armies of the United States, but I am in command here, and as you are not safe where you are standing, and I am responsible for your personal safety, I order you to come down."

General Horatio G. Wright, Commander of the VI Corps

coincidence, on the very day that President Lincoln paid a visit to the fort. Confederate sharpshooters spotted Lincoln and opened fire, making this the only time a sitting United States president was ever fired upon in battle—and while Lincoln was unhurt, the skirmish made history. Early is reported to have told his staff officers later that night, "We didn't take Washington, but we scared Abe Lincoln like hell." (You can visit the partially restored fort at 13th and Quackenbos Streets NW, in the northern part of the city.)

The next bullet aimed at the president, however, found its mark: Days after the war ended at Appomattox, actor John Wilkes Booth came into Lincoln's box at Ford's Theatre and fired a gun into the back of his head. Lincoln died the next morning at Petersen House, the home just across the street from the theater, and Vice President Andrew Johnson stepped into the role of commander in chief.

After the war, with a rocky Reconstruction in progress and a struggling South working to get back on its feet, Congress found time to focus on a local matter: In 1871, at the urging of a contingent of Washington's most powerful citizens, the legislative body passed an act that united George-town, Washington, and Washington County into a single entity. A territorial governor would run the newly joined county, and Alexander Robey Shepherd—head of the DC Board of Public Works—took the position of vice-chair, quietly wielding the governor's power while the generally disinterested Governor Henry D. Cooke focused his attentions elsewhere.

With "Boss" Shepherd in charge, new plans began to fix the city's ailing finances and continue the capital's development. Clean-up projects emerged as Shepherd filled in the crumbling Washington Canal and mandated the construction of 157 miles of paved roads and sidewalks, closed sewers, gas lines, and water mains, modernizing the city at a rapid pace. When Governor Cooke resigned, President Grant appointed Shepherd to the post. Congress, however, considered him too extravagant, investigating his finances and going so far as to abolish the office of governor to keep him from raiding his overextended budget any further.

By the 1880s, Washington's population had soared from about 20,000 people in the late 1830s to upwards of 177,000 residents. Washington showed all of the good and bad signs of growth: electric lighting in the White House, new streets, streetlights, and sidewalks, and a sewage system —but the people were divided into the "haves" and "have nots," with the comfortable middle class filling the city's new suburbs, and the poor and homeless spending their nights on the streets or in alleys to dodge the watching eyes of law enforcement. As the city began to look forward to its first centennial, the next step was clear: The nation's

The transformation from an unhealthy, unsightly city to a city of fine, graded, graveled and paved, and shaded streets, well lighted at night, an extended system of sewerage, an efficient water supply, miles upon miles of shade, and acres upon acres of beautiful parks . . . was the most surprising and complete. . . . The presiding genius of this great transformation and improvement was Alexander R. Shepherd. **From Centennial History of the City of Washington, DC by Harvey W. Crew and William Bensing Webb, 1892**

capital needed a makeover to accommodate its continually swelling population, a project that would clean up its streets, tear down the slums, and turn the groaning city into the proud national center it needed to be.

Begin your tour near the White House at the Renwick Gallery, which is just a block from the Farragut West Metro station.

1. Renwick Gallery. This building, designed by architect James Renwick Jr., originally housed the American and European art collection of William Corcoran, a Washington banker. Modeled in the French Second Empire style—inspired by the Tuileries addition to the Louvre in Paris—the building opened in 1873, but Corcoran's collection outgrew the space by 1897, and in the 1950s it was slated for demolition. First Lady Jacqueline Kennedy led the effort to rescue it, convincing the

Jacqueline Kennedy saved the Renwick Gallery from demolition.

government to turn it over to the Smithsonian. In 2014, the gallery began another extensive renovation to renew its infrastructure and enhance its historic features; the gallery is expected to reopen in late 2015. 1661 Pennsylvania Avenue at 17th Street NW, (202) 633-1000, americanart.si.edu/ renwick. Daily 10–5:30; closed Christmas. Free. Metro: Farragut West. DOWNTOWN.

2. Eisenhower Executive Office Building. The "Old" Executive Office Building currently houses the Offices of the Vice President, Management and Budget, and the National Security Council, but this strikingly detailed French Second Empire building originally provided offices to the State, War, and Navy Departments when it was completed in 1888. Just as impressive on the inside as its facade might suggest, this building's rich history is worth the extra effort to schedule a tour. 17th Street and Pennsylvania Avenue NW, (202) 395-5895, www .whitehouse.gov/history/eeobtour. Tours Saturday morning by reservation; call Tuesday or Wednesday 9–noon to schedule. Free. Metro: Farragut West. DOWNTOWN.

3. Corcoran Gallery of Art. One of the world's finest three-century collections of American art, this gallery showcases the tastes and acquisitions of its founder, Georgetown banker William Wilson Corcoran. The gallery relocated to this building in 1897, and its curators continue to expand the collection with works by contemporary artists. 500 17th Street NW, (202) 639-1700, www.corcoran .org. The gallery is closed for renovation until late 2015; check the website for reopening dates and new hours. Metro: Farragut North. DOWNTOWN.

4. National Museum of African American History and Culture. This new addition to the Smithsonian Institution's network of museums will open in 2016, on a five-acre tract near the Washington Monument. Its collection will include objects from across the country, assembled to tell the story of the African American experience in the United States. The museum will also address the impact of this race's struggle on freedom movements around the world. Today the museum's welcome center can be found on the second floor of the National Museum of American History. Daily 10–5:30, closed Christmas. Free. Metro: Federal Triangle. DOWNTOWN.

5. Old Post Office Tower. Washington's first skyscraper, this 315-foot tower was the first building in DC to have its own electric power plant—but its architecture, described by the *New York Times* as "a cross between a cathedral and a cotton mill," drove its detractors to slate it for demolition just fifteen years after its construction. Enter Nancy Hanks and the DC Preservation League, who started a preservation movement on the already-deemed "Old" Post Office's behalf. They won their fight, and the tower stood for decades as the Old Post Office Pavilion, a delightful center that featured shops, restaurants, tours of the tower, and yes, even stamps. The Old Post Office Tower is closed until spring 2016 for a massive renovation to transform it into a hotel. 1100 Pennsylvania Avenue NW, (202) 289-4224, www.nps. gov/opot. Metro: Federal Triangle. DOWNTOWN.

Why do I show my interest in this splendid structure here? Because at this time of the year, before setting, the disk of the Sun cuts through the Old Post Office tower, to the south of Pennsylvania Avenue. I doubt that this phenomenon is accidental. Indeed, it may go a long way toward explaining why the Old Post Office . . . was allowed to survive the bulldozers . . . To watch this temporary eclipse of the Sun by the vertical masonry of the tower is itself a deeply mystical experience.
From *The Secret Architecture of Our Nation's Capital* by David Ovason, 2002

6. Ford's Theatre National Historic Site.

On April 14, 1865, an actor with southern sympathies shot President Abraham Lincoln while he watched a performance of *Our American Cousin* on the stage below. John Wilkes Booth then leapt from the president's box above the stage, landed onstage, and broke his leg before fleeing from the theater. Lincoln died early the next morning. It's not often that we have the opportunity to stand in the footsteps of a president and his assassin, but we can do so here, making the historical impact of this local theater even more profound for visitors. A major renovation—including construction of a new museum about the assassination—was completed in 2009. 511 10th Street NW, (202) 426-6924, www.nps.gov/foth. Daily 9–5; closed Christmas. Free; visitors must have time entry tickets, available daily at the box office beginning at 8:30 or

The Old Post Office is closed for renovations as it becomes a hotel.

Suddenly there was realization. It came to the audience and all with inflaming demand for retribution. In an instant there was great confusion. Practically as one, the audience stood up. A few persons rushed to the lobby to ascend to the box. Scores climbed over the footlights and poured onto the stage. Pistols were drawn. Search for Booth then commenced.

W. J. Ferguson, who was working backstage at Ford's Theatre the night Lincoln was shot.

7. Petersen House. The "house where Lincoln died" was a boarding house owned by German-born tailor William Petersen and the closest residence to Ford's Theatre. Lincoln breathed his last in a bed too small for his great height, at 7:22 on the morning of April 14, 1865, just a week after General Lee surrendered to General Grant at Appomattox and ended the Civil War. Your short tour includes the bedroom in which Lincoln died, as well as the parlor where Mary Todd Lincoln and her son, Robert, waited throughout the anguished

Petersen House is best known as the House Where Lincoln Died.

night to hear of the president's fate. 516 10th Street NW, (202) 426-6924, www.nps.gov/foth. Daily 9:30–5:30, closed Christmas. Free. Metro: Gallery Place/Chinatown. DOWNTOWN.

8. General Ulysses S. Grant Memorial. Dedicated to the victorious general in chief of the Union forces during the last years of the Civil War, this impressive memorial was designed and sculpted by Henry Merwin Shrady—a man so committed to his task that he actually joined the National Guard for several years to experience military life firsthand before he began his design. At 252 feet long and 71 feet wide, this is the largest and most elaborate piece of statuary in Washington, befitting the man who brought home the triumph that reunited the nation. The memorial, dedicated in 1922, features Grant on his warhorse, Cincinnati, with Confederate and Union troops on each side of him and grand symbols of war at each corner. In front of the Capitol at 1st Street and Penn-

Mr Shrady's modelling of horses in action has hardly been equaled by any other sculptor.
From *The American Review of Reviews* by Albert Shaw, 1922

Hundreds of visiting children are dwarfed by the larger-than-life Grant Memorial.

sylvania Avenue NW, (202) 426-6841, www.nps.gov/nama. Always open. Free. Metro: Capitol South or Union Station. CAPITOL HILL.

9. James A. Garfield Monument. Elected president in 1880, Garfield served just four months before his assassination in 1881 by Charles J. Guiteau, a delusional office-seeker. The monument, sculpted by John Quincy Adams Ward, was unveiled May 12, 1887, and depicts Garfield in bronze at the top, with three allegorical figures—student, warrior, and statesman—that represent phases of the president's career. Capitol Building grounds, in the circle at 1st Street W and Maryland Avenue (near the U.S. Grant Memorial), (202) 225-6827, www.aoc.gov/cc/grounds/art_arch/garfield.cfm. Always open. Free. Metro: Capitol South. CAPITOL HILL.

The Peace Monument completes the trio of sculptures in front of the Capitol.

10. Peace Monument. Built to commemorate naval deaths at sea during the Civil War, the Peace Monument is the third in the group of sculptures in front of the Capitol. At the top of the memorial, Grief weeps while hiding her face against History; at lower levels, Victory demonstrates strength by holding a laurel wreath and an oak branch, while the two infants are Mars (god of war) and Neptune (god of the sea). Peace, the last figure, faces the Capitol. Capitol Building grounds, 1st Street NW and Pennsylvania Avenue, (202) 225-6827, www.aoc.gov/cc/grounds/art_arch/peace.cfm. Always open. Free. Metro: Capitol South. CAPITOL HILL.

11. Library of Congress. This is *America's* library, the largest in the world and the research arm of

Congress and the American people. Established in 1800 with $5,000 and housed in the Capitol until it burned in 1814, the library's losses were replenished by Thomas Jefferson, who sold his fifty years' accumulation of books to Congress for $23,950 to provide new resources for the governing body. In 1864, Librarian of Congress Ainsworth Rand Spofford sponsored the Copyright Law of 1870, which required all copyright applicants to send two copies of their work to the library. The resulting avalanche of printed materials led Congress to order the construction of a new building. Today, more than 32 million volumes reside here in three buildings, as well as nearly 106 million documents, photographs, and audio and video recordings. The Library offers hour-long tours of the Thomas Jefferson Building throughout the day,

The Library of Congress holds more than 32 million books.

I have long been sensible that my library would be an interesting possession for the public, and the loss Congress has recently sustained, and the difficulty of replacing it, wile our intercourse with Europe is so obstructed, renders this the proper moment for placing it at their service.
Thomas Jefferson's letter to President James Madison, September 24, 1814

where you can see the splendid Main Reading Room and learn about the building's art, architecture, and collections. 101 Independence Avenue SE, (202) 707-8000, www.loc.gov. Jefferson Building: M–Sa 8:30–4:30; Madison Building: M–F 8:30 a.m.–9:30 p.m., Sa 8:30–5; Adams Building: M, W, Th 8:30 a.m.–9:30 p.m., T, F, Sa 8:30–5. All buildings closed Sunday and federal holidays. Free. Metro: Capitol South. CAPITOL HILL.

12. Smithsonian Castle. A funny thing happened to the United States in 1836: British scientist James Smithson named his nephew as the

Smithsonian Castle opened to the public in 1855.

beneficiary of his estate, noting that if the nephew died without heirs, the estate should go to the United States, "to found at Washington, under the name of the Smithsonian Institution, an establishment for the increase and diffusion of knowledge among men." What's odd about this uncommon generosity is that Smithson had never been to the U.S., or had even known anyone here. But when the nephew died without an heir, the estate—more than $508,318 in 1830s dollars—arrived at the U.S. Treasury. Congress established a Secretary of the Smithsonian and began construction of this first building, which originally contained an art gallery, lecture hall, library, chemical laboratory, natural history laboratory, and science museum. Smithsonian Castle opened in 1855, and today the building houses the Smithsonian Information Center and a cafeteria-style restaurant. The Smithsonian Institution now includes 19 museums and attracts 26.8 million visitors annually. 1000 Jefferson Drive SW, (202) 633-1000, www.si.edu. Daily 8:30–5:30. Free. Metro: Smithsonian (Mall exit). DOWNTOWN.

13. Bureau of Engraving and Printing. When the United States began issuing paper currency in 1861, the printing operation originally ran in the basement of the Treasury Building. By 1877, the Bureau of Engraving became the sole producer of all U.S. currency, and today it prints billions of Federal Reserve Notes (currency) every year, as well as security documents like portions of U.S. passports, military ID cards, and materials for Homeland Security. You'll see millions of dollars being printed during your tour—but resist the urge to ask for samples. The tour guides have heard it all. 14th and C Streets SW, (202) 874-2330, (866) 874-2330,

It is an interesting subject of speculation to consider the motives which actuated Smithson in bequeathing his fortune to the United States of America to found an institution in the city of Washington. . . . He is not known to have had a single correspondent in America. . . . Living at a time when all Europe was convulsed with war, when the energies of nations, the thoughts of rulers, and the lives of millions were devoted to efforts for conquest or to perpetuate despotism, he turned to the free American Republic, where he could discern the germs of rising grandeur, the elements of enduring prosperity, and the aspirations of coming generations.
From *James Smithson and His Bequest* by William Jones Rhees, 1880

Historical Tours

www.moneyfactory.gov. Tours Sep–Mar, M–F 9–10:45 and 12:30–2; Apr–Aug, M–F at 9–10:45, 12:30–3:45, 5, and 6; get tickets at booth on Raoul Wallenberg Place, weekdays beginning at 8 (lines form as early as 5:30). Free. Metro: Smithsonian. NATIONAL MALL.

14. Washington Monument. Construction of this monolith's 555 feet and 5⅛ inches began in 1848, but it was 1884 before funds and available marble came together to permit its completion. This tribute to our first president saw construction in two phases: the first 55 feet from 1848 to 1856, and the rest from 1876 to 1884, after the Civil War ended and new influxes of funds arrived. When construction resumed, the original marble source in Maryland could no longer provide the material, so there's a slight color change at the 152-foot mark, when Massachusetts marble replaced it. This first of the National Mall monuments is still the tallest, and it will remain so by city law. On the National Mall, between 15th and 17th Streets, (877) 444-6777 to reserve tickets in advance, www.nps.gov/wamo. Tours daily 9–5; closed July 4 and Christmas. Free; get tickets at Washington Monument Lodge, on 15th Street on the grounds of the monument, beginning at 8:30; tickets are often gone by 9; lines begin to form at 7. Metro: Smithsonian. NATIONAL MALL.

15. Lincoln Memorial. Proposed in 1867 and finally completed in 1922, this icon of memorial design was the brainchild of architect Henry Bacon, sculptor Daniel Chester French, and artist Jules Guerin. Colorado Yule marble and Tennessee pink marble define the exterior, with steps and terrace walls of pink Massachusetts granite. The interior

Washington, DC

. . . Many people throughout the Union felt deeply mortified and chagrined at the neglect of Congress to fittingly express its appreciation of the great services of the first soldier and the first President of the Republic, and as a consequence a popular movement was attempted by which it was hoped to raise the money necessary to carry out the design of erecting a suitable monument to the memory of Washington. The plan was to raise if possible a popular subscription of $1 from each family throughout the United States, and by 1812 about $35,000 was thus raised.

From Centennial History of the City of Washington, DC by Harvey W. Crew, William Bensing Web, John Wooldridge, 1892

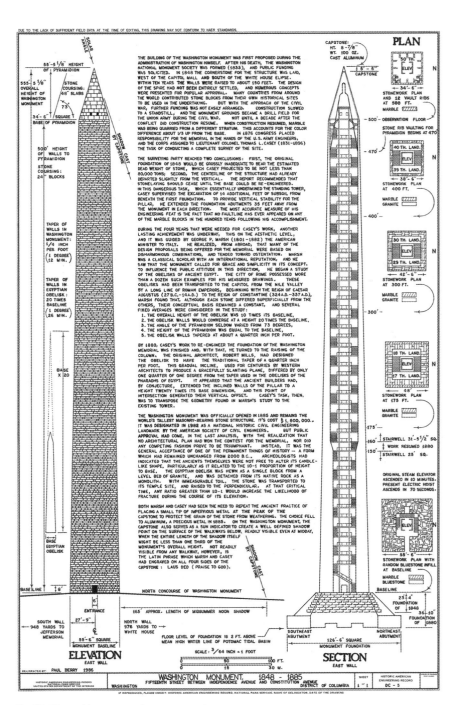

The Washington Monument took years to complete.

Abraham Lincoln received a place of honor at the end of the National Mall.

stone came from Indiana, Georgia, Tennessee, and Alabama, completing the monument's 1,292 vertical feet from base of foundation—and all together, the materials weigh an astonishing 76 million pounds. You've come to admire Lincoln, but while you're here, stop and read the 256 words of the Gettysburg Address chiseled into the marble walls. This speech endures as the most famous presidential oration in history for good reason: its brilliantly concise and heartfelt summation of the Civil War's significance to lasting democracy in America. On the National Mall, 23rd Street between Independence and Constitution Avenues, (202) 426-6842, www.nps.gov/linc. Daily 8–midnight. Free. Metro: Smithsonian. NATIONAL MALL.

Living Richly in 1894

Washington had its share of fabulously wealthy residents, one of whom made his fortune on a commodity nearly every household sought: beer. Christian Heurich, owner of the Christian Heurich Lager Beer Brewery, became one of the area's richest citizens and its second largest landowner, as well as the largest private employer in the capital city. With his wealth, he built this late Victorian home on New Hampshire Avenue NW using poured concrete and reinforced steel, creating the city's first fireproof house and a structure so impressive that the neighbors called it the "Brewmaster's Castle."

Brewmaster's Castle.

A stop at the Christian Heurich House Museum reveals its interior opulence, with its elaborately carved wood fireplaces, extensive use of gold leaf, and the brass, marble, and onyx staircase that greets you in the foyer. Much of the furniture is original to the house, giving visitors a clear idea of just how the top one-tenth of one percent lived in turn-of-the-twentieth-century Washington. 1307 New Hampshire Avenue NW, (202) 429-1894, www.heurichhouse.org. Tours Th–Sa by reservation only; complete the form on the website. $5 per person. Metro: Dupont Circle. NORTHWEST.

Tour 3: 1901–1950

From L'Enfant to McMillan: Washington Takes Shape

As the twentieth century arrived and Washington celebrated its own bicentennial, Congress and the city's residents had no illusions about what the capital had become. Slums ringed the Capitol Building, traffic clogged the streets, visible poverty and congestion were everywhere, and people who could afford to do so fled by railroad, cable car, and electric streetcar for the new suburbs in Anacostia, Takoma Park, Chevy Chase, and beyond.

In the ensuing years since Pierre L'Enfant completed the original design for America's capital, the needed funds and motivation to continue its execution had never surfaced. Now, with the population growing at an alarming rate, Washington looked like a grimy city in which the federal government just happened to work. The grand plan for a capital showplace had fallen by the wayside.

In 1901, the Senate chose to make the city's appearance and growth a top-level priority. The Senate Park Improvement Commission of the District of Columbia, headed by Senator James McMillan of Michigan, took on the task of planning the next phase in beautifying and enriching Washington. The committee's members included some of the greatest architects of the day: Frederick Law Olmsted Jr., who was renowned for his creation of city parks; sculptor Augustus Saint-Gaudens, best known for his colossal "Standing Lincoln" in Chicago and the Robert Gould Shaw Memorial

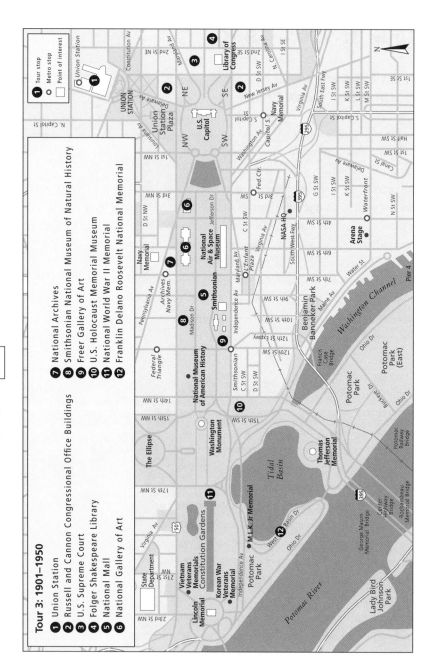

Tour 3: 1901–1950

1. Union Station
2. Russell and Cannon Congressional Office Buildings
3. U.S. Supreme Court
4. Folger Shakespeare Library
5. National Mall
6. National Gallery of Art
7. National Archives
8. Smithsonian National Museum of Natural History
9. Freer Gallery of Art
10. U.S. Holocaust Memorial Museum
11. National World War II Memorial
12. Franklin Delano Roosevelt National Memorial

1. Tour stop
   Metro stop
   Point of interest

in Boston; Charles F. Kim, a Beaux-Arts architect who would go on to design New York's Penn Station; and Daniel Burnham, known for his role as Director of Works for the 1893 World's Fair.

The committee began with L'Enfant's original plan, and added their familiarity with the grandest capitals of Europe—London, Paris, and Rome—to consider the most appropriate ways to proceed. At the time, a movement called City Beautiful had come to prominence in North American architecture, with the concept of using majestic buildings and monuments to beautify cities and improve quality of life, promoting a sense of harmonious social order among urban populations.

With all of these influences in mind, the McMillan Commission moved forward to remove the slums near the Capitol and replace them with government buildings, monuments, and memorials. They moved buildings out from in front of the Capitol and the Washington Monument, and created the National Mall that L'Enfant had specified more than one hundred years earlier. Beyond the mall, they ordered the construction of Union Station, the nation's largest railroad station and the kind of transportation hub that would be worthy of the nation's capital. Commission member Burnham received the contract for the station's design.

Construction reached completion in 1922, culminating in the dedication of the Lincoln Memorial. Washington finally had a Capital District it could show off with pride, with sweeping green lawns, marble and granite tributes to great leaders, and modern technologies for transportation and daily life.

The object of the present investigation is to prepare for the city of Washington such a plan as shall enable future development to proceed along the lines originally planned—namely, the treatment of the city as a work of civic art—and to develop the outlying parks as portions of a single well-considered system.

From *The Improvement of the Park System of the District of Columbia*, Report of the Senate Committee on the District of Columbia; Report of the Park Commission, 1902

Historical Tours

From the air, the transportation network through Union Station becomes clear.

Congress took another step to mandate a higher aesthetic in Washington's overall design: In 1910, an Act of Congress created the Commission of Fine Arts, a council of "well-qualified judges," including artists, architects, and administrators, who advise government agencies throughout the District of Columbia on design issues. The design of new monuments, memorials, and even coins and medals go through this esteemed commission, ensuring that all projects meet a defined set of criteria for quality and historical appropriateness throughout the district.

In the meantime, Washington continued its enormous growth—and with more people came more conflicts over race, gender, politics, and rights. Demonstrations in the streets and even riots became part of the district's fabric, as Washington became the nation's sounding board, the city in which every citizen wanted to be heard. In the 1920s, as the black community worked to rise above the issues of discrimination around them, they coalesced in the U Street neighborhood, turning this area into a thriving hub of business activity and nightlife and attracting some of the nation's most prominent black citizens to its clubs, restaurants, and shops. Even with this progress, however, segregation continued to hound children in city schools and black patrons in white restaurants.

With the Great Depression came demonstrations by the hungry and the unemployed, and the efforts by Franklin Roosevelt's New Deal to put people to work in ways that would benefit the entire nation. Roosevelt's Works Progress Administration gave jobs to more than eight million citizens across the country, with a significant percentage assigned to the capital city. Reconstruction and improvement of public utilities, completion of buildings including the National Gallery of Art and the Supreme Court, and landscaping of green areas all took place from 1935 through 1943. By then, America was once again at war. And as women streamed into Washington looking to fill the jobs abandoned by men-turned-soldiers, the city's highest courts began making decisions that would change America once again, mandating equal rights for every citizen regardless of the color of his skin.

Begin your tour by taking the Metro to Union Station, at Massachusetts Avenue NE and 1st Street. You may wish to start your day with breakfast at one of the many restaurants inside.

Washington was not depression proof for everybody, but better for other people because of the government. People doing domestic work were out of work. It certainly affected us. It wasn't as bad as other cities. I don't remember bread lines. . . . Everybody wasn't so bad off. Some of them worked for the government and they still had their jobs. We worried about losing the house. We'd open a can of fruit and have it for two nights. It was a struggle. I would wear my cousin's clothes.
Janet Kasdon Lobred from *Growing Up in Washington, D.C.*, **Historical Society of Washington, DC**

Historical Tours

1. Union Station. The largest railroad station in the country when it opened in 1907, Union Station served Washington as its transportation hub for half a century. The station's Presidential Suite, used by President Taft first and by many presidents that followed, through Eisenhower (and by George H. W. Bush in 1991), also welcomed Queen Elizabeth II, King Albert I of Belgium, King Prajadipok of Siam, Queen Marie of Romania, and King Hassan II of Morocco. As flying became the preferred travel method, the station fell into a decline until Congress passed the Union Station Redevelopment Act in 1981, calling for a plan for the station's commercial reawakening. The $160 million renovation produced a multiuse facility with 130 shops and restaurants, while it continues to serve as an Amtrak hub. 50 Massachusetts Avenue NE at 1st Street, (202) 289-1908, www .unionstationdc.com. M–Sa 10–9, Su 12–6. Free. Metro: Union Station. CAPITOL HILL.

When it opened, Union Station was the largest railroad hub in the country.

2. Cannon and Russell Congressional Office Buildings. Before these two buildings were constructed, members of Congress had to rent their own office space or borrow committee rooms in which to work, a costly and inefficient system at best. In the early 1900s Congress acquired the land for these two buildings, and Architect of the Capitol Edward Clark planned the modified Beaux-Arts design—attractive, but not so much that the buildings overshadow the Capitol. The Cannon House Office Building, the older of the two, was named for Congressman Joseph "Uncle Joe" Cannon of Illinois, the much-respected Speaker of the House from 1903 to 1911. Cannon served in Congress from 1873 until 1923 (except for two terms), and he himself laid the cornerstone of this building on April 15, 1906.

Joseph Cannon.

The Senate staff moved into the "Old Senate Building" on March 5, 1909, and it quickly became the site of some of the most controversial hearings in American history. Senators heard evidence on the sinking of the *Titanic* in 1912, the Army-McCarthy controversy in 1954, the Watergate scandal in 1973–74, the 1987 Iran-Contra scandal, and the 1991 Clarence Thomas confirmation. In 1972, Congress changed the building's name to honor Richard Brevard Russell, a Democratic senator from Georgia who founded and led the Conservative Coalition in Congress from 1937 to 1963. Cannon House Office Building: Independence Avenue and 1st Street SE; Russell Senate Office Building: Delaware and Constitution Avenues NE, (202) 224-6827, www.aoc.gov/cc. Open to the public during normal office hours while Congress is in session. Free. Metro: Capitol South or Union Station. CAPITOL HILL.

Historical Tours

The U.S. Supreme Court relocated to this building in 1935.

Washington, DC

We recently entered its sacred precincts in company with an irreverent Western lawyer. After gazing around a moment, he exclaimed: "I don't wonder at that decision in the Dred Scott Case. Why! What a potato hole of a place, this! The old men ought to be got up above ground where they can breathe fresh air and see real daylight once in a while!"
From *The Supreme Court in United States History* by Charles Warren, 1922

3. U.S. Supreme Court. Imagine, if you will, the highest court in the United States meeting in a small room in the basement of the Capitol building—and then, in an upward movement, relocating to a single ground floor room on the Capitol's north wing. Such was the nomadic existence of the U.S. Supreme Court in 1929, when Chief Justice and former President William Howard Taft argued to Congress that the court should have its own building. Congress saw the light, and the court relocated for the last time in 1935, settling into the building that would become an icon for ultimate justice across the country. Self-guided exhibits on the main level are open to the public, giving us the opportunity to experience the corridors of law for ourselves. 1 1st Street NE at East Capitol Street, (202) 479-3000, www.supremecourtus.gov. M–F, 9–4:30. Free. Metro: Union Station or Capitol South. CAPITOL HILL.

4. Folger Shakespeare Library. Using their personal collection of the works of William Shakespeare, Standard Oil chairman Henry Clay Folger and his wife, Emily Jordan Folger, established this library in 1932. It now houses the world's largest collection of Shakespeare's printed works, as well as many other rare materials dating between 1500 and 1750. 201 East Capitol Street SE, (202) 544-4600, www.folger.edu. M–Sat 10–5, Su 12–5, closed all federal holidays. Free. Metro: Capitol South or Union Station. CAPITOL HILL.

5. National Mall. A key component of the L'Enfant design but largely forgotten throughout the nineteenth century, the National Mall became the centerpiece of the McMillan Plan in 1901. It took seven years to transform this congested area into the "grand avenue" the Senate Commission envisioned—including the removal of an entire

The publicque walk . . . will be agreeable and convenient to the whole city which . . . will have an easy access to this place of general resort and all long side of which may be placed play house—room of assembly—academmies and all such sort of places as may be attractive to the larned and afford divertion to the idle.

Pierre L'Enfant's description of the Mall in a letter to President George Washington, August 1791

The McMillan Plan transformed the National Mall.

railroad station—but today the National Mall is America's front lawn, a place where citizens gather to express their opinions, campaign for their causes, celebrate national triumphs, and welcome a new president. The Smithsonian Institution's many museums line the avenues along the eastern mall, while memorials to great figures in American history are the principal features of its western half. The Trust for the National Mall has taken on the daunting task of raising funds to complete a long overdue restoration of monuments, reflecting pools, turf, and foundations, as well as a rehabilitation of Constitution Gardens. You will see the positive results of this effort throughout your visit to the mall. Between Constitution and Independence Avenues from the Capitol (1st Street) to the Lincoln Memorial (23rd Street), (202) 426-6841, www.nps. gov/nama. Always open. Free. Metro: Smithsonian. NATIONAL MALL.

6. National Gallery of Art. When this quintessential gallery of art opened in 1941, it was originally based on the extensive collection of banking magnate Andrew W. Mellon. A philanthropist who began purchasing art in the 1920s, Mellon always intended to use his collection to form a gallery of art for the nation—and true to his word, he left the collection to the United States on his death in 1937, along with trust funds for the construction of a gallery. Just as Mellon expected, major donations of art followed from collectors throughout the country. Most recently, in 1999, the Gallery opened an outdoor garden of modern and contemporary sculpture in the six-acre block adjacent to its West Building. Between 3rd and 7th Streets on Constitution Avenue NW, (202) 737-4215, www.nga.gov. M–Sa

Washington, DC

10–5, Su 11–6; closed Christmas and New Year's Day. Free. Metro: Smithsonian. NATIONAL MALL.

The WPA completed construction of the National Gallery of Art.

7. National Archives. Before 1935, each agency of the federal government was expected to preserve its own documents, no matter how critical they might be to national history or public record. When the flaws in this system became obvious, Congress acted to centralize preservation of the nation's most important records and documents. The National Archives hold the Declaration of Independence, the U.S. Constitution, and Bill of Rights, as well as the Magna Carta, the record of the Louisiana Purchase, the Emancipation Proclamation, and thousands of other documents. See the nation's most famous documents when you visit the Rotunda for the Charters of Freedom, including treasures selected from the Archives' substantial vaults. 8th Street and Pennsylvania Avenue, (866)

272-6272, www.archives.gov. Open daily 10–5:30, closed Thanksgiving Day and Christmas Day. Free. Metro: Archives/Penn Quarter. NATIONAL MALL.

8. National Museum of Natural History. One of the first museums in the institution, this 1.5 million-square-foot facility was constructed exclusively to house more than 125 million natural science specimens and cultural artifacts. If the real African elephant in the lobby is not enough to grab your attention, visit the Sant Ocean Hall, an immersion

Don't miss the Sant Ocean Hall at the Smithsonian Museum of Natural History.

experience in the sights, sounds, and creatures of the unseen world undersea, where a 45-foot-long model of a North American right whale dominates your first impression and a detailed, highly visual exhibit hall explains the evolutionary process over 3.5 billion years. Need more reason to visit? The Hope Diamond resides in a glass case upstairs. 10th Street and Constitution Avenue NW, (202) 633-1000, www.mnh.si.edu. Daily 10–5:30; closed Christmas. Free. Metro: Smithsonian. NATIONAL MALL.

9. Freer Gallery of Art. Charles Lang Freer, a railroad car manufacturer from Detroit, gave to the United States his collection of paintings and sculpture from Asia and by twentieth-century American artists, as well as the funds to build a museum for them. The collection includes more than 1,300 works by James McNeill Whistler, as well as works by Winslow Homer, John Singer Sargent, and John

In November 1958, jewelry merchant Harry Winston sent the Hope Diamond to the Smithsonian Institution by mail from New York. The package, weighing 61 ounces, was insured for $1 million; Winston paid $145.29 for postage. "It's the safest way to mail gems," he said.

The Freer Gallery of Art features the work of Asian and American artists.

Twachtman, major nineteenth- and twentieth-century American artists. (In fact, it was Whistler who advised Freer personally to build a collection of Asian art.) When this gallery opened in 1923, it was the first Smithsonian museum to house fine art. Jefferson Drive and 12th Street SW, (202) 633-1000, www.asia.si.edu. Daily 10–5:30; closed Christmas. Free. Metro: Smithsonian. NATIONAL MALL.

10. U.S. Holocaust Memorial Museum. During World War II, the National Socialist (Nazi) Party in Germany targeted groups they perceived to be racially inferior: Jews, Roma (Gypsies), Poles, Russians, Communists, Jehovah's Witnesses, and homosexuals, among others. Between 1933 and 1945, Nazis imprisoned and killed nearly two out of every three Jews in Europe as part of a process they called the Final Solution. This museum tells the story of the Holocaust and the Jewish experience in Nazi-dominated Europe, using modern museum design and display methods that make this a fascinating experience as well as a moving one. 100 Raoul Wallenberg Place, (202) 488-0400, www.ushmm.org. Daily 10–5:20 with extended hours in spring; closed on Yom Kippur and Christmas. Free. Metro: Smithsonian. NATIONAL MALL.

11. National World War II Memorial. Dedicated in 2004, this extensive and deeply affecting memorial honors the sixteen million people who served in the U.S. armed forces during World War II. The design, with its inclusive enclosure and many symbolic elements, succeeds in commemorating everyone who served: the 400,000 who died in the war, the millions more who fought in the European and Pacific theaters, and the millions of Americans who

Everything about the museum is powerful; even the architecture was intentionally designed to give visitors a sense of life under the Nazis. The stark brick and limestone exterior is supposed to remind people of a German factory. Inside James Freed's design seems flawed: Rooms do not always have right angles, the windows are different sizes, the floor is fractured, and the interior brick walls are uneven in shape and color, as were the bricks used in the crematoria. Freed intentionally wanted to convey the sense of a world gone awry.

From Jewish Virtual Library website: www.jewishvirtual library.org/

supported the war from home. While you visit, stop at the visitor center and add your loved one's name to the World War II registry. 17th Street between Constitution and Independence Avenues, (202) 619-7222, www.nps.gov/wwii. Daily 8–midnight. Free. Metro: Smithsonian. NATIONAL MALL.

Take some time to walk and absorb the National World War II Memorial.

12. Franklin Delano Roosevelt Memorial. In four chronological chambers, one for each of the four terms of the Roosevelt presidency, this memorial's contemporary design uses representational sculpture and art to tell the stories of the Great Depression, the New Deal, World War II, and Roosevelt's imposing presence, including a sculpture of him in a wheeled chair. Quotes from the longest running presidency in American history help us understand what encouraged the nation to re-elect Roosevelt again and again: Despite his partial paralysis and failing health, his words continued to inspire a nation desperately in need of hope and change.

Among American citizens there should be no forgotten men and no forgotten races.
From President Roosevelt's address at Howard University, Washington, DC, October 26, 1932

The Franklin Delano Roosevelt Memorial uses scupture to tell the story of the Great Depression.

On the western edge of the Tidal Basin, (202) 426-6841, www.nps.gov/frde. Daily 8–midnight; closed Christmas. Free. Metro: Smithsonian. NATIONAL MALL.

Side Trip: Washington National Cathedral

Plans to construct a national center for Catholic worship began as far back as 1792, but no cornerstone was laid until 1907—and while the cathedral's first chapel opened in 1912, it would be 1990 before this extraordinary celebration of gothic architecture would see full completion. In the interim, the National Cathedral served as the site of services for peace at the end of World War I, a gathering place for monthly services throughout World War II, and the final resting place of President Woodrow Wilson, whose tomb resides here—along with the tombs of Helen Keller, Admiral George Dewey, Bishop Satterlee, and two of the architects who designed the building: Henry Vaughan and Phillip Frohman.

With 231 stained glass windows, 112 gargoyles, and 288 stone angels watching over its visitors, the cathedral is one of the most visually arresting houses of worship in the world. Be sure to stop at the gift shop after your tour. 3101 Wisconsin Avenue NW, (202) 537-6200, www.nationalcathedral.org. M–F 10–5:30, Sa 10–4:30, Su 8–6:30 (tours on Sunday from 1–2:30 only). $10 adults, $6 children 5–12, seniors, military, or students; free to children 4 and under. Metro: Tenleytown/AU. CLEVELAND PARK.

Tour 4: 1951–2000

Washington's New Focus: Civil Rights, Science, and the Arts

With nonviolent demonstrations throughout the southern states and new leadership focusing the nation's attention on issues of civil rights, Washington began to move toward integration. Mary McLeod Bethune, founder of the National Council of Negro Women, rose to prominence as the first black woman to hold a leadership position on the federal level, heading the Division of Negro Affairs of the National Youth Administration. Just around the corner from Bethune's home in the Council House, Mary Church Terrell—at the tender age of eighty-six—brought a lawsuit against Thompson's

Civil rights became the primary issue in Washington by 1963.

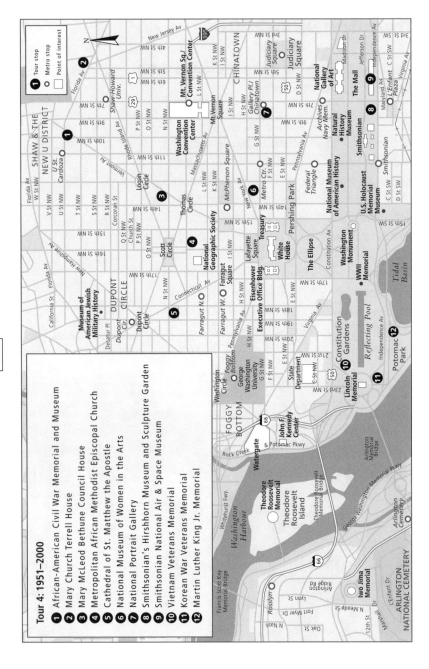

Washington, DC

Tour 4: 1951–2000

1. African-American Civil War Memorial and Museum
2. Mary Church Terrell House
3. Mary McLeod Bethune Council House
4. Metropolitan African Methodist Episcopal Church
5. Cathedral of St. Matthew the Apostle
6. National Museum of Women in the Arts
7. National Portrait Gallery
8. Smithsonian's Hirshhorn Museum and Sculpture Garden
9. Smithsonian National Air & Space Museum
10. Vietnam Veterans Memorial
11. Korean War Veterans Memorial
12. Martin Luther King Jr. Memorial

Restaurant and led the fight to end segregation in Washington's dining establishments. When the courts ruled in her favor, the decision signaled a sea change in the treatment of African-Americans in the nation's capital.

As public segregation began to crumble in Washington, the nationwide issue took on a new face and new leadership. On August 28, 1963, a young reverend from Atlanta, Georgia, stood on the steps of the Lincoln Memorial and delivered a speech that would change America, describing a dream in which his children would be judged "not by the color of their skin, but by the content of their character." Dr. Martin Luther King Jr., gave a voice and a new hope to an underserved population, bringing his message of change to every household in the country. President Lyndon Johnson responded by working with King for passage of the Civil Rights Act, signing the act into law in 1964.

While social issues rose to the fore in the early 1960s, new themes emerged in Washington: John F. and Jacqueline Kennedy worked to increase the importance of the arts and sciences throughout the nation, beginning here in the capital city. Kennedy's term of office as our thirty-fifth president would end abruptly with his assassination in Dallas on November 22, 1963, but the influence of his ideas and those of his first lady would linger for many years to come. The Smithsonian added the American Art Museum and National Portrait Gallery in 1968, and in 1971, the John F. Kennedy Center for the Performing Arts became the premier venue for theater, dance, and music in the United States. The National Aeronautics and Space Administration (NASA) reached for the moon and succeeded

No memorial oration or eulogy could more eloquently honor President Kennedy's memory than the earliest possible passage of the civil rights bill for which he fought so long. We have talked long enough in the country about equal rights. We have talked for one hundred years or more. It is time now to write the next chapter, and to write it in the books of law.
From President Lyndon B. Johnson's speech before a joint session of Congress, November 27, 1963

The Kennedy Center is the nation's premier performing arts center.

in 1969, and the Smithsonian embraced the excitement of space travel by opening the National Air and Space Museum several years later.

With broader ideas came a broader spectrum of residents. In recent years, Washington's population reflects not only America's demographics but those of the world as a whole. Latino, Asian, European, and African residents have revitalized the city center, creating ethnic neighborhoods with fascinating shops, restaurants, and cultural activities of their own, while giving the city its invigorating sense of international connection. Today's Washington goes beyond the traditional "melting pot" concept with which the country identified in the twentieth century to embrace a new profile in which individuality wins out over conformity. The result is a bright fabric of cultures, styles, and colors—a delightful adventure for visitors who venture beyond the National Mall and into the city's many neighborhoods.

Begin your tour north of downtown in Washington's vibrant U Street neighborhood. Take the Metrorail to the U Street/African-American Civil War Memorial station.

1. African-American Civil War Memorial and Museum. This one-of-a-kind memorial remembers more than 200,000 soldiers who fought as the U.S. Colored Troops in the Civil War. The detailed sculpture, rich with symbolism, includes the name of every soldier inscribed on the Wall of Honor. Don't miss the museum, just around the corner at

The first colored troops did not receive any pay for eighteen months, and the men had to depend wholly on what they received from the commissary, established by General Saxton. A great many of these men had large families, and as they had no money to give them, their wives were obliged to support themselves and children by washing for the officers of the gunboats and the soldiers, and making cakes and pies which they sold to the boys in camp.
From *Reminiscences of My Life in Camp with the 33rd United States Colored Troops* by Susie King Taylor, 1988

Historical Tours

The African-American Civil War Memorial recognizes the 200,000 U.S. Colored Troops.

1200 U Street—it's loaded with documents and artifacts from the war, and hosted by some of the most knowledgeable and engaging museum staff members we have encountered anywhere. 1925 Vermont Avenue NW, (202) 667-2667, www.afroam civilwar.org. Memorial always open. Museum Tu–F 10–6:30, Sa 10–4, Su 12–4. Free. Metro: U Street/ African-American Civil War Memorial. U STREET.

If judged by the depths from which they have come rather than by the heights those blessed with centuries of opportunities have attained colored women need not hang their heads in shame.

—Mary Church Terrell

Washington, DC

2. Mary Church Terrell House. As you walk toward your next stop, turn on T Street and pass the home once owned by one of the quieter leaders in the fight for civil rights. Local integration laws written in 1872 and 1873 required all eating-place proprietors "to serve any respectable, well-behaved person regardless of color, or face a $1,000 fine." The new District Code rewritten in the 1890s, however, eliminated this statute, opening a loophole that allowed restaurant owners to refuse service to people of color. On February 28, 1950, eighty-six-year-old Mary Church Terrell and several colleagues entered Thompson Restaurant and requested seating. When they were refused service, Terrell and friends marched out of the restaurant and on to the District of Columbia courthouse, where they filed a lawsuit against Thompson. As the suit dragged through three years of court proceedings, Terrell organized her neighborhood and targeted other restaurants with sit-ins, picketing, and boycotts, making a quiet but firm statement about the rights of African-Americans and about the antiquated, unjust laws. By the time her case was heard in court in 1953, Terrell had disrupted business enough throughout the area that the court saw her point, ruling in her favor and putting an end to segregation in District restaurants. 326 T Street NW, no phone. www.nps

.gov/history/nr/travel/civilrights/dc2.htm. Not open to the public. Metro: U Street/African-American Civil War Memorial. U STREET.

3. Mary McLeod Bethune Council House National Historic Site. Founder of the National Council of Negro Women in 1935, Bethune lived in this house and used it as Council headquarters from 1943 through 1955. Here she developed programs that advanced the interests of African-American women, and received heads of state and government officials—including First Lady Eleanor Roosevelt and Madame Pandit, the United Nations delegate from India. Today the National Archives for Black Women's History resides in this house. 1318 Vermont Avenue NW, (202) 673-2402, www.nps .gov/mamc. Daily 9–5, last tour starts at 4; closed Thanksgiving, Christmas, and New Year's Day. Free. Metro: McPherson Square. U STREET.

Whether it be my religion, my aesthetic taste, my economic opportunity, my educatonal desire, whatever the craving is, I find a limitation because I suffer the greatest known handicap, a Negro—a Negro woman.
—Mary McLeod Bethune

4. Metropolitan African Methodist Episcopal (AME) Church. Built in the late 1800s, this continuously operating church was organized by parishioners of two congregations that broke away from white churches. It quickly became a center of community events, whether people gathered for a concert, family celebration, civil rights meeting, or a Sunday worship and fellowship. Abolitionist and national speaker Frederick Douglass chose this parish for his own worship while he lived across the river in Anacostia; his funeral in 1895 drew thousands to this church from all over the area. 1518 M Street NW, (202) 331-1426, www.metropolitan amec.org. M–Sa 10–6; services Su at 7:45 and 11. Free. Metro: Farragut West. DUPONT CIRCLE.

5. Cathedral of St. Matthew the Apostle. The official cathedral for the Archdiocese of Washington, this house of worship has been lauded for its combination of Byzantine and Romanesque architecture and its exquisite mosaics. Many remember this church as the site of President John F. Kennedy's funeral on November 25, 1963; today, a memorial marks the location of the casket. More recently, Pope John II celebrated mass here in 1979, and each year the Supreme Court justices and members of Congress gather here for the Red Mass, which requests divine guidance for people of the legal professions. 1725 Rhode Island Avenue NW, (202) 347-3215, www.stmatthewscathedral.org. Open to the public for mass; see schedule on Web site. Metro: Farragut North or Dupont Circle. DUPONT CIRCLE.

6. National Museum of Women in the Arts. Founded in 1981 in the private home of Wilhelmina Holladay, the museum moved into this Renaissance Revival–style building—a former Masonic temple—in 1983. The extensive collection includes works by Mary Cassatt, Berthe Morisot, Elaine de Kooning, and Frida Kahlo, among many others. 1250 New York Avenue NW, (800) 222-7270, www.nmwa.org. M–Sa 10–5, Su 12–5; closed Thanksgiving, Christmas, and New Year's Day. Adults $10, students and seniors (ages 60+) $8, ages 18 and under free. Metro: Metro Center. DOWNTOWN.

7. National Portrait Gallery. Located in the former Patent Office, one of the oldest public buildings in Washington, this collection presents portraits of people who have influenced our society, past and present. The extensive gallery includes works by John Singleton Copley, Winslow Homer, John

. . . We felt that there was a whole gap in the history of art that needed filling, that absolutely was a legitimate part that was missing. So always from the start it wasn't really in a sense that women hadn't been treated right, we certainly found that out later on, but it was more the fact that we wanted to be—to contribute to the history of art. . . .
Oral history interview with Wilhelmina Holladay, August 17 to September 23, 2005, Archives of American Art, Smithsonian Institution

Singer Sargent, Childe Hassam, Georgia O'Keeffe, Edward Hopper, Jacob Lawrence, Robert Rauschenberg, and many others. The permanent exhibition of America's presidents includes portraits of all forty-four presidents to date, with multiple images of many of them—you are certain to recognize the portraits of George Washington and Abraham Lincoln, as well as the caricatures of twentieth-century presidents by artist Pat Oliphant. 8th and F Streets NW, (202) 633-8300, www. npg.si.edu. Daily 11:30–7; closed Christmas. Free. Metro: Gallery Place/Chinatown. DOWNTOWN.

8. Hirshhorn Museum and Sculpture Garden. Opened in 1974, this collection of modern and contemporary art contains works from the late nineteenth century through the early 2000s. Take a thirty-minute impromptu tour with a guide to get a sense of the gallery's three floors, or explore on your own—and don't miss the bi-level Sculpture Garden. Independence Avenue at 7th Street SW, (202) 633-1000, hirshhorn.si.edu. Daily 10–5:30; closed Christmas. Free. Metro: Smithsonian. NATIONAL MALL.

With the opening of the Hirschhorn Museum, modern art arrived in Washington.

At the Smithsonian National Air & Space Museum, you can see the *Spirit of St. Louis, Glamorous Glennis,* and many other famous aircraft.

9. National Air & Space Museum. Walk into the entrance hall of this expansive museum and count the number of air- and spacecraft you know by name: The 1903 *Wright Flyer,* the *Spirit of St. Louis,* the Apollo 11 command module *Columbia,* Chuck Yeager's *Glamorous Glennis,* and many others hang suspended from the ceiling in this multi-story gallery. Twenty-two exhibition halls tell stories of the invention of flight, the development of aircraft, and the greatest moments in air and space exploration—and the Albert Einstein Planetarium and IMAX Theater each present several shows daily to extend your experience. Independence Avenue at 6th Street SW, (202) 633-1000, www .nasm.si.edu. Daily 10–5:30; closed Christmas. Free. Metro: Smithsonian. NATIONAL MALL.

Washington, DC

10. Vietnam Veterans Memorial. How to honor the men and women who gave their lives in the war in Vietnam, the most controversial war of the twentieth century? Young architect Maya Lin took on this challenge in a competition for the memorial's design—and while her choice became nearly as controversial as the war itself, the Vietnam Veterans Memorial is now hailed as one of Washington's most affecting. Lin's concept succeeds in putting politics aside, honoring the sacrifice of each individual: More than 58,000 names of those who died in the conflict are inscribed on the wall, and a hush falls over visitors as they walk its length. On any day at any time of year, you'll see tributes to loved ones laid beneath their names; these are collected daily, catalogued, and preserved in a facility in Andover, Maryland. Constitution Garden, at Constitution Avenue and Henry Bacon Drive, (202) 426-6841, www.nps.gov/vive. Daily 8–midnight; closed Christmas. Free. Metro: Foggy Bottom. NATIONAL MALL.

11. Korean War Veterans Memorial. From June 1950 through July 1953, American military forces under the banner of the United Nations fought alongside South Korean citizens to combat Communist-allied forces from North Korea. This memorial, dedicated in 1995, commemorates the loss of 54,246 lives in the war on the 28th Parallel, employing nineteen statues of men on the field of war in uniforms that represent all of the American armed forces. Stop here in the evening, when details become especially sharp in the memorial's dramatic lighting. Independence Avenue at Daniel

The Vietnam memorial is a place where something happens within the viewer. It's like reading a book. I purposely had the names etched ragged right on each panel to look like a page from a book. . . . I also wanted remembering the past relevant to the present. Some people wanted me to put the names in alphabetical order. I wanted them in chronological order so that a veteran could find his time within the panel. It's like a thread of life.
Maya Lin quoted in the UC Berkeley Berkeleyan, March 15, 1995

The Korean War Memorial is at its best at night.

French Drive SW, (202) 426-6841, www.nps.gov/kowa. Daily 8–midnight; closed Christmas. Free. Metro: Foggy Bottom. NATIONAL MALL.

12. Martin Luther King Jr. Memorial. Positioned across the Tidal Basin from the Jefferson Memorial, the monument to the leader of the civil rights movement uses the landscape to focus on three themes of King's life: justice, democracy, and hope. The contemplative space brings together water, stone, and trees as symbolic elements, combining to capture the spirit of the leader's message as well as his actual words, deeds, and ideals. On the northeast corner of the Tidal Basin, at Independence Avenue and West Basin Drive. (888) 484-3373, www.mlkmemorial.org. Daily 8–midnight, closed Christmas. Metro: Smithsonian or Foggy Bottom. TIDAL BASIN.

MLK Memorial

Staying, Eating, and Touring in Washington, DC

Your trip to Washington can stir your sense of national patriotism, widen your eyes with the beauty and enormity of its monuments and memorials, excite your imagination with its mix of cultures and the murmur of dozens of languages, and make you giddy with the sense of being so close to the world's most powerful government.

What it will *not* do is save you money. While the vast majority of museums, monuments, and historic sites in Washington are free to visit, a trip to Washington is far from a budget vacation: Hotel rooms inside the Beltway average in the hundreds of dollars per night. Whether you choose the historic Hay-Adams Hotel or the Quality Inn on the outskirts of downtown, you need to be prepared for the reality of big-city pricing.

The good news is that you can save a few dollars by skipping the car rental and taking advantage of Washington's excellent mass transportation to get to the most popular areas. The Washington Metropolitan Area Transit Authority runs a network of underground trains—the **Metrorail**—that are clean, quiet, dependable, and inexpensive. Purchase a SmarTrip card from the vending machines at any Metro stop or online at smartrip.wmta.com for as little as $10.00, and you'll save $1 on every ride to any of the forty-two stops to the National Mall, the major museums, and trendy neighborhoods like Foggy Bottom, Penn Center, and Adams-Morgan. **Metrobus,** the above-ground transportation system, takes you beyond the Metrorail stops on the major

You'll find plenty to see and do on "America's Main Street," Pennsylvania Avenue.

streets, bringing you close to your final destination. Visit www.wmata.com for route maps, fees, and details about riding both the subway and the buses.

If you're spending the day touring the National Mall area and beyond, we highly recommend the **Old Town Trolley Tours** (www.trolleytours. com/washington-dc). You'll see the orange and green trolleys all over the National Mall area and at the National Cathedral, as well as in Arlington Cemetery. Your one-day ticket price (in 2015, $39 for adults, $29 for children 4–12, with significant discounts if you buy your tickets online in advance) buys you hop-on, hop-off privileges for the entire day, reducing the amount of time you will spend walking from one memorial to another—and by the end of the day, you'll be pleased to have the ride instead of walking 2 miles back to your starting point. Trolley drivers offer a well-informed narrative about the city's history and points of interest.

You may see the red **DC Circulator** buses, especially if you spend time near Union Station or Georgetown, on the Mall, or in the City Center area of 7th Street SW. The Circulator runs along these three specific routes daily from 7:00 a.m. to 9:00 p.m., at a cost of only $1 per ride (a $3 one-day pass buys you unlimited riding for the whole day). The buses arrive every ten minutes. View the routes and rate information at www.dccirculator.com.

One last reason to choose mass transit over your own vehicle: Parking around the Mall, downtown, in Georgetown, and in other areas within metropolitan DC is a veritable nightmare. Parking spaces on the street are crowded by early morning, and parking garages are few and far between. If you'd rather not spend your day in Washington looking for a place to park, leave your car at your hotel—or at home.

SLEEPING IN A SLICE OF HISTORY

All of your favorite hotel chains are here, from luxury brands like Sofitel, Intercontinental, and JW Marriott to the Choice Hotels group (Comfort, Quality, EconoLodge, and so on), Doubletree, Hampton, Hilton, Best Western, and many more. Before you book one of these with an online travel discount site, however, be sure you've chosen a hotel that's close to a Metro stop or bus route, and check a map to see if it's in an area that matches your expectation of comfort. For example, the room that's under $100 per night could be so far out on the edge of town that you won't be able to take advantage of mass transit. Another caveat: Like all big cities, Washington has its marginal areas, and the lowest priced hotels may put you right in the middle of one of these neighborhoods. Watch out for this if you're booking a nonrefundable reservation on Priceline or Hotwire, where you're committed to a hotel before you know what venue you've bought.

Here are some rules of thumb as you choose your accommodations:

- Most of the city is considered "northwest" because of its location in reference to the Capitol. Northwest includes most of downtown, Foggy Bottom, Georgetown, Adams-Morgan, and much more.
- You'll find residential areas with somewhat less expensive hotels (but still $150 or higher per night) in the southwest quadrant.
- The northeast has much less expensive motels, but you will be well outside of the tourist areas and you may not find accommodations as comfortable, or restaurants as plentiful.

If you're really on a budget, consider staying outside the city proper, where you'll find all of your favorite hotel chains within a 15-mile drive of the city (still inside the Interstate 495 Beltway). You can park your car at a train station and take the MARC commuter rail into the city from Maryland (www.mta maryland.com), or the Virginia Railway Express from many areas south of the city (www.vre.org).

The closer you are to the National Mall, the more luxurious and expensive the hotels become, but these establishments can be worth the cost if you're looking to create a special, memorable trip to the capital city. Steeped in history and the first choice of visiting dignitaries from all over the world, these are the hotels you glimpse in movies about Washington politics and in news coverage of inaugural balls. Here are some with names you may recognize:

Hay-Adams Hotel. Since 1928, this recently renovated establishment has hosted some of Washington's most prominent citizens and visitors, from Ethel Barrymore and Charles Lindburgh in the 1930s to President Barack Obama and his family in the weeks before the 2009 inauguration. With 125 rooms and twenty suites, this first-class boutique hotel offers amenities most of us have never thought about, like Italian bed linens and bath towels, a Bose CD music system and CDs in each room, and your choice of morning newspaper. Best of all, you have a view of the White House just across the street. 16th and H Streets NW (Lafayette Square), (202) 638-6600, www .hayadams.com. DOWNTOWN.

Henley Park Hotel. Constructed as the Tudor Apartments in 1918, this distinctively embellished building was transformed into a boutique hotel in 1982, but the renovation preserved the 119 marble gargoyles and the brilliantly chromatic stained glass. The rich decor continues into the ninety-six stately guest rooms, where amenities are as modern as business visitors require. 926 Massachusetts Avenue NW, (202) 638-6638, www .henleypark.com. PENN QUARTER.

Hotel Monaco (a Kimpton Hotel). This 183-room boutique hotel skillfully combines the traditional and the contemporary for an eclectic, visually stunning lobby and ultra-comfortable guest rooms. Designed by Robert Mills, architect of the Washington Monument, this hotel prides itself on its guest services—plush terrycloth robes, a hosted wine reception every evening, a fitness center, and fine dining at the Post-Moderne Brasserie. You'll

Staying, Eating, and Touring

feel like a very sophisticated guest in these beautifully appointed quarters. 700 F Street NW, (202) 628-7177, (877) 202-5411, www.monaco-dc.com. PENN QUARTER.

Marriott Renaissance Mayflower Hotel. Designed in the European Beaux-Arts style with old world elegance, this circa-1925 hotel is the largest luxury accommodation in the District of Columbia—and while its decor says ultra-traditional, it offers a newly renovated fitness center and a restaurant for fine dining. A separate entrance is reserved for visiting foreign diplomats and U.S. government officials. The 657 rooms include seventy-four lush suites, as well as more standard rooms for tourists and business travelers. 1127 Connecticut Avenue NW, (202) 347-3000, www.marriott.com/hotels/travel/wassh-renaissance-mayflower-hotel. Metro: Farragut North. DOWNTOWN.

Marriott Renaissance Washington, DC Hotel. The closest hotel to Washington's Convention Center, this new, modern option features energy-efficient utilities and construction and high-speed Internet in every guest room. Bold, bright colors and comfortable furniture accent the guest rooms, and each bed provides a deluxe mattress, down comforter, and soft linens to lull you to sleep. 999 9th Street NW, (202) 898-9000, www.marriott.com/hotels/travel/wasrb-renaissance-washington-dc-hotel. PENN CENTER.

Phoenix Park Hotel. In the shadow of the Capitol Building, this Irish-style hotel feels like a country estate, with its highly polished wood, eighteenth-century-style prints in its draperies and wallpaper, and cozy rooms. The Dubliner Pub serves an

authentic plate of corned beef and cabbage, and the bar fills up early in anticipation of live Celtic folk music in the evening. It's no wonder that diplomats, businesspeople, and tourists alike enjoy this comfortable lodging. 520 North Capitol Street, (202) 638-6900, www.phoenixparkhotel.com. Metro: Union Station. DOWNTOWN.

Watergate Hotel. You know you want to—and yes, beginning in 2015, you can stay in the hotel where a 1972 break-in became the frayed knot that unraveled a presidency. The hotel is undergoing an extensive renovation that began in late 2014, but it maintains its distinctive curved shape and its four round buildings, which hold office space, apartments, shops, and restaurants as well as the hotel. Beyond the scandal, residents of the Watergate complex have included former Vice President Bob Dole and his wife, former Senator Elizabeth Dole; former Secretary of State Condoleezza Rice; and a former White House intern named Monica Lewinsky. 2650 Virginia Avenue NW, (202) 965-2300, www.the watergatehotel.com. Currently closed for extensive renovation (reopening 2015). FOGGY BOTTOM.

The Watergate Hotel is a famous landmark in Foggy Bottom.

Staying, Eating, and Touring

Willard Intercontinental Hotel. Built in 1850 and completely renovated in 1904—and again between 1968 and 1986—the Willard set the original standard for grand hotels from the day it opened its doors. It has hosted every American president since Zachary Taylor, and it even became the hiding place for Abraham Lincoln in the days before his 1861 inauguration, when assassination threats forced the president-elect into police protection. Woodrow Wilson held the first meetings of the soon-to-be League of Nations here, and Martin Luther King Jr., stayed here in the days before he delivered his "I Have a Dream" speech. Today the posh accommodations feature a luxury spa, two excellent restaurants, and afternoon tea served daily in the Peacock Gallery promenade. 1401-09 Pennsylvania Avenue NW, (202) 628-9100, www.ihg.com/intercontinental/hotels/gb/en/washington/washa/hoteldetail. DOWNTOWN.

When it opened in 1850, the Willard Hotel set the gold standard for Washington hotels.

WHERE TO EAT WHILE TOURING WASHINGTON

While you're walking on and around the National Mall, you're sure to get hungry—but it may be tougher than you'd expect to find a quality dining experience close to all the tourist action. Washington is renowned for its excellent restaurants, but few are near the National Mall: The streets that lead immediately north, south, and west from the mall are remarkably devoid of restaurants beyond the occasional Potbelly or Corner Bakery Cafe (two national chains that offer good-quality sandwiches and salads), or the very upscale fine dining establishments in the luxury hotels. At the other end of the spectrum, the National Park Service provides refreshment concessions in several central locations on the National Mall—but you may want something more interesting than hot dogs and chips.

Happily, there are opportunities for a good, reasonably priced family meal right on the Mall, thanks to the foresight of the Smithsonian Institution and the National Gallery of Art. Six Smithsonian museums offer quick, easy, and tasty options; all with plenty of seating so you can rest your tired feet while you enjoy your meal. Not to be outdone, the National Gallery's restaurants take the museum meal to the level of an experience, matching many of their offerings to the nationality of the current exhibition. Here's the scoop on museum dining:

Atrium. One of four options in the National Museum of Natural History, the Atrium serves natural and sustainable foods—including natural beef burgers, hot dogs, and pizza as well as rotisserie chicken. M–F 11–3.

The Castle Café in Smithsonian Castle offers tasty, healthy lunch options.

Castle Café. This is a good place to find freshly made sandwiches, salads, bottled drinks, and snacks, including fresh fruit and healthy alternatives. Inside Smithsonian Castle Information Center, 8:30–5.

Constitution Café. One of two cafeteria-style restaurants in the National Museum of American History, this first-floor establishment offers a considerable selection of family favorites. 10–5.

Courtyard Café. Sandwiches and salads made to order, as well as daily soups and desserts, make this a pleasing choice. When weather permits, the café's open-air extension, the Portico Café, serves meals, pastries, coffee, wine, beer, and cocktails outside. Smithsonian American Art Museum, National Portrait Gallery, 11:30–6:30.

Cafe Natural. Also in the National Museum of Natural History, Cafe Natural gives you that shot of caffeine you're craving in a variety of espresso and cappuccino drinks, as well as sandwiches, soups, and salads, There's an ice cream and espresso bar in the museum as well, and outdoor carts offer hot dogs, sodas, ice cream, and Dippin' Dots. 10–5.

McCafé. Find wraps and *panini* sandwiches, pastries, and beverages at this quick stop. When weather permits, McCafé hosts an outdoor kiosk with McDonald's quarter-pound burgers, hot dogs, and ice cream. Smithsonian Air & Space Museum, 10–5.

Mitsitam Native Foods Café. *Mitsitam* means, "Let's eat!" in the Piscataway native language, and you'll want to try many dishes at this Native American–themed café. Foods from five regions of the Western hemisphere include seasonal soups, buffalo burgers, fry bread, tamales, roasted turkey, and much more. The Mitsitam Espresso Bar offers pastries, casual meals, and snacks, as well as fair trade Tribal Grounds Coffee, grown by indigenous farmers and imported by the Eastern Band of the Cherokee. National Museum of the American Indian, 11–5.

Stars and Stripes Café. This is the ground floor cafeteria in the National Museum of American History, with much the same fare as the Constitution Café upstairs. 11–3, extended hours when crowds warrant.

Wright Place Food Court. Your fast-food favorites are here: McDonald's, Boston Market, and Donatos Pizzeria. Smithsonian Air & Space Museum, 10–5.

In addition to the Smithsonian's many eateries, the National Gallery of Art offers three restaurants and a sophisticated snack bar:

Cascade Café. Named for its proximity to the gallery's cascade waterfall, this restaurant offers a daily Chef's Table selection of specials, as well as sandwiches of unusual creativity and an annual picnic menu. M–Sa 11–3, Su 11–4.

Espresso & Gelato Bar. Sandwiches with European flair, crisp green salads and nineteen flavors of gelato make this quick stop more interesting than most. M–Sa 10–4:30, Su 11–5:30.

The Garden Café, in the West Building next to the ground-floor galleries, provides a menu selected to complement current exhibitions. An elegant buffet and à la carte dishes reflect specific nationalities, with as much flair and design as the works of art themselves. Bring you appetite and plan a leisurely lunch. M–Sa 11:30–3, Sun 12–4; dessert menu only for concerts on selected Sundays, 4–6.

Pavilion Café. Enjoy the view of the Sculpture Garden while you munch on a freshly prepared sandwich, salad, or specialty pizza. M–Sa 10–5, Su 11–6.

POPULAR DOWNTOWN CENTERS FOR DINING AND SHOPPING

When you're ready to venture away from the city's many historic sites and into the whirl of shopping and dining, be sure to stop at these commercial centers—each of which makes its home in an inventively converted historic building. You'll find a balanced blend of chic boutiques, souvenir emporia, big-city chain stores, and both locally owned and national restaurants, in settings that are as much fun to admire as they are to explore.

Union Station. In the 1980s, a $160 million renovation of this 1908 former railroad station transformed the building into a grand, tastefully appointed multipurpose facility. Today Union Station houses more than 130 shops and restaurants. There's an extensive food court on the lower level with everything from burgers and pizza to sushi, including Greek and Cajun specialties, smoothies, and all kinds of desserts and snacks. You'll also find a wide range of quick food items in the corridors leading to the Amtrak trains, and a market with fresh fruit and groceries. Union Station features several finer dining options as well. 50 Massachusetts Avenue NE, (202) 289-1908, www.unionstationdc.com. CAPITOL HILL.

Center Café, the elevated restaurant on the mezzanine in the middle of the Main Hall, is the first dining establishment you'll see as you enter the building. A raw bar and a wide selection of quesadillas and entrées ranging from lobster ravioli to roasted chicken make this a good choice for dinner. The breakfast menu features vanilla-bean French toast and hand-mixed granola with strawberries. Street level, Main Hall. (202) 898-0051, www.arkrestaurants.com. M–F: 8 a.m.–9:30 p.m. Sa–Su: 11:30–9:30. CAPITOL HILL.

Thunder Grill offers an extensive menu of seafood prepared with imagination and style—try the honey-chili-glazed salmon or the blue-cornmeal-crusted swordfish—and a nice variety of entrées including barbecued beef brisket, red-chili chicken potpie, and a bison sirloin steak. Dine at lacquered tables with wicker chairs in the East Hall, or enter the dramatically decorated restaurant for a quieter meal. Street level, Main Hall. (202) 898-0051, www .arkrestaurants.com. Lunch and dinner, 11:30 a.m.–10 p.m. Brunch Sa–Su 11:30 a.m.–4:00 p.m. CAPITOL HILL.

Center Café in Union Station offers fine dining three meals a day.

East Street Cafe brings the flavors of East Asia to Union Station, with a carefully chosen menu of specialties from China, Japan, the Philippines, Singapore, Thailand, and Vietnam. Choose from curries, unusual fried rice dishes, barbecue flavors, and mild and spicy dishes. Mezzanine level, (202) 371-6788, www.eaststreetcafe.com. M–F 11–8, Sa–Su 12–6. CAPITOL HILL.

Capitol City Brewing Company is a polished brass and glossy wood-paneled microbrewery with an appealing menu of straight-ahead pub favorites. Start your meal with a cup of stout-ale chili, then choose from burgers and sandwiches, heaped-high salads, a beer-and-bourbon glazed pork chop, fish-and-chips, or a dynamic chicken and ribs combo. The big copper brewing tanks in the center of the bar remind you to try at least one of the pub's signature brews. 1100 New York Avenue NW, (202) 628-2222, www.capcitybrew.com. M–Th and Su 11 a.m.–12 midnight. F–Sa 11 a.m.–1 a.m. DOWNTOWN.

Relax with a microbrew at Capitol City Brewing Company.

Rasika showcases regional dishes and cooking methods from India, with small plates that allow you to try a number of different styles and flavors in one sitting. This is no ordinary Indian restaurant—Rasika is rated one of the top 20 restaurants in the country by Zagat, and its chef received the 2014 James Beard Award as the best chef in the Mid-Atlantic region. You'll also enjoy the international wine list, selected for optimal pairing with the menu. 633 D Street NW, (202) 637-1222, www.rasikarestaurant.com. Lunch M-F 11:30–2:30, dinner M–Th 5:30–10:30, Sa–Su 5–11. PENN QUARTER.

The Ronald Reagan Building and International Trade Center offers many options for a quick bite or a full-course dinner. The food court's eighteen choices range from burgers and chicken to Japanese selections, a delicatessen, and a Cajun grill, along with ice cream, specialty coffees, and snacks. 1300 Pennsylvania Avenue NW, (202) 312-1300, www.itcdc.com. M–F 7–7, Sa 11–6, Su 12–5 (Mar through Aug only). Closed New Year's Day, Easter Sunday, Thanksgiving and Christmas Day. Metro: Federal Triangle. DOWNTOWN.

Market to Market offers an alternative to the crowds at the food court: a café with a daily selection of forty-five fine foods including a carving station with hams, turkeys, and chickens sliced to order, and additional Asian specialties that change daily. Eat at tables in the market, or take your meal with you. (202) 289-4710. Breakfast also served; closes daily at 6, closed weekends Oct–May.

Fogo de Chayo offers a dining experience you would normally find in Brazil: Once you've helped yourself to more than 30 items on the expansive salad and side dishes bar, the gaucho chefs begin serving you fresh-sliced, fire-roasted meats whenever your plate is empty. Select from 16 different cuts, including beef, chicken, and pork, and enjoy sides including warm cheese bread, polenta, carmelized bananas, and a host of others. 1101 Pennsylvania Avenue NW, (202) 347-4668, www .fogodechao.com. Lunch M–F 11:30–2:30, dinner M–Th 5–10, F 5–10:30, Sa 4:30–10:30, Su 4–9:30. **Note:** Free for children 6 and under, half price for children 7–12.

DINING NEAR GEORGETOWN'S HISTORIC SITES

Well known for its busy M Street lined with stores, markets, restaurants, and the occasional dab of history, Georgetown attracts thousands of visitors every day throughout the spring, summer, and fall—and it's no wonder, with the concentration of interesting things to see and do in this relatively small community. You'll visit the Old Stone House and the Chesapeake and Ohio Canal on your walking tour, both of which are smack in the middle of Georgetown's most popular section. When you're ready for a great meal, you won't go wrong with any of these highly rated, glowingly recommended establishments.

Blue Duck Tavern. Great food prepared simply—by braising, roasting, or smoking—makes this neighborhood tavern compelling, comfortable, and satisfying. It's not every menu that offers a 12-hour roasted suckling pig, steelhead trout from Alaska, or grits with smoked Gouda cheese as a side dish, but you will find all of these in season and many more fresh, hearty dishes to tempt your palate. 1201 24th Street NW at M Street, (202) 419-6755, www.blueducktavern.com. Daily breakfast, 6:30–10:30 a.m., lunch (or brunch Sa-Su) 11:30 a.m.–2:30 p.m., dinner 5:30–10:30 p.m. GEORGETOWN.

La Chaumière. Remember when French cuisine was . . . well, French? La Chaumière celebrates the old-fashioned flavors that made French cooking the epitome of haute cuisine. Choose salmon *en croute* (in puff pastry) with champagne-dill sauce,

Visitors have no trouble finding great restaurants and shopping in Georgetown.

or duck breast with black currant sauce, or come on Tuesday for crepes filled with lump crabmeat and mushrooms in a champagne cream sauce. Do you crave escargot? The snails are swimming in butter the old-fashioned way, just for you. 2813 M Street NW, (202) 338-1784, www.lachaumiere dc.com. M–F: 11:30 a.m.–2:30 p.m., 5:30–10:30 p.m. Sa: 5:30–10:30 p.m. Closed Sunday. GEORGETOWN.

Seasons. Start your day with breakfast at the Four Seasons Hotel, and your day will be perceptibly brighter. Seasons maintains its focus on seasonal and regional ingredients, offering the freshest foods in tantalizing combinations of flavors. Choose traditional meals like New England corned-beef hash with poached eggs or buttermilk pancakes with Vermont maple syrup, or go rogue with a Mediterranean egg-white omelet with olives, spinach, tomatoes, and feta—or Virginia ham over an open croissant, with scrambled eggs and fontina. A strangely alluring selection of granolas, cereals, and oatmeal with blueberry compote complete the one-of-a-kind menu. 2800 Pennsylvania Avenue NW, (202) 944-2000, www.fourseasons .com/washington/dining/seasons.html. M–F: 6:30–10 a.m., Sa–Su: 7–10:30 a.m., Sunday brunch 10:30 a.m.–2:30 p.m., Sa lunch 10:30 a.m.–2 p.m. Sa lunch only, no dinner hours. GEORGETOWN.

DOING IT UP DC STYLE: THE TOP RESTAURANTS IN WASHINGTON

How to select the best restaurants our nation's capital has to offer? With literally hundreds of fine dining experiences from which to choose, we had to make some tough choices. Here are some of the standouts that win rave reviews from locals and visitors alike:

Marcel's. If you're looking for the old-school fine dining experience you see in your favorite classic movies, this is the place to go. Jackets are required in this posh establishment, where you will find a maitre d' ready to seat you at a white-linen-draped table, and a staff that redefines the concept of efficient service. The prix fixe menu changes daily, but you can expect a range of brilliantly prepared French and Belgian dishes from which you will choose four, five, six, or seven courses. You can also expect a three-figure bill for your extraordinary meal. 2401 Pennsylvania Avenue NW, (202) 296-1166, marcelsdc.com. M–Th 5:30–10, F–Sa 5:30–11, Su 5:30–9:30. FOGGY BOTTOM.

Fiola. The menu changes daily at this fairly new Italian restaurant, to take advantage of the freshest ingredients available locally. Choose from the four-course or six-course menu or order a la carte, and enjoy an elegantly prepared meal of exciting variations on dishes you thought were familiar. From From prawns and mussels mingled with sea urchin to a veal chop nestled in prosciutto, you are sure to taste something startling here. 601 Pennsylvania Avenue NW, (202) 628-2888, www. fioladc.com. Lunch M–F 11:30 a.m.–2:30 p.m., dinner M–Th 5:30–10:30, F 5:30–11:30, Sa 5 p.m.–12 a.m., closed Sun.

The Lafayette and Off the Record at Hay-Adams Hotel. Top off the wonderful cuisine at the Lafayette with drinks at Off the Record, and you'll have a classic Washington evening in high style. The natural light in the Lafayette dining room gives you a full view of the artfully prepared entrées—from pan-seared Pennsylvania pheasant to sautéed veal paillard. The relaxed atmosphere and extensive wine list at Off the Record, serving light fare from 11:30 a.m. to 11 p.m., receive accolades from critics and customers alike. 800 16th Street NW, (202) 638-6600, www.hayadams.com. Off the Record: Su–Th: 11:30 a.m.–12 midnight; F-Sa 11:30 a.m.–12:30 a.m. Lafayette: Breakfast M–F: 6:30–11 a.m., Sa–Su: 7–11 a.m. Lunch M–Sa: 11:30 a.m.–2 p.m. Sunday brunch: 11:30 a.m.–2 p.m. Dinner: M–F: 5:30–10 p.m., no dinner weekends. DOWNTOWN.

Old Ebbitt Grill. A Washington mainstay since 1856, this world-famous eatery was a favorite of Presidents Ulysses S. Grant and Theodore Roosevelt, and it continues to live up to its reputation: You never know who you will run into while dining at this political hot spot. The traditional grill fare is sourced from local farms in season and from native regions for meats and fish; you *must* sample the highly touted oysters. 675 15th Street NW, (202) 347-4800, www.ebbitt.com. M–F: 7:30 a.m.–1 a.m. Sa–Su: 8:30 a.m.–1 a.m. Bar is open until 2 a.m. Su–Th, and until 3 a.m. F–Sa. DOWNTOWN.

The Palm. If you've pictured yourself tucking into a steak in a classic DC steakhouse, you've come to the right place. Aged steaks and jumbo lobsters are two of the most popular features on the delightful menu, and the service is unsurpassed. 1225 19th Street NW, (202) 293-9091, www. thepalm.com/Washington-DC. M–F: 11:45–10, Sa: 5:30–10, Su: 5–9. No lunch weekends. GOLDEN TRIANGLE.

Taberna Del Alabardero. The Spanish government designated this restaurant the "Best Spanish restaurant outside of Spain," a well-deserved accolade for this delightful change of pace. You'll find traditional Spanish favorites, but always with added originality and flair—like strip-loin paella with an aioli crust, boneless beef oxtail with wild rice, or marinated partridge with Andalusian couscous and fava beans. Carved dry-cured meats are a particular delicacy. Stop for a drink and decidedly creative tapas-style small plates. 1776 I Street NW, (202) 429-2200, www.alabardero.com. Lunch

M–F: 11:30 a.m.–2:30 p.m., dinner M-Th: 5:30–
10:30; F–Sa 5:30–11, Su 5:30–10. WORLD BANK.

Zaytinya. The earthy flavors of Greece, Lebanon,
and Turkey are reconceived as dazzling nibbles
by Chef José Andrés at this stylish Penn Quarter
mezzeteria. Mezze (small plates) pick up where
tapas leave off, with a whole new host of tangy,
savory bites to delight your senses. 701 9th Street
NW, (202) 638-0800, www.zaytinya.com. Su–M:
11:30 a.m.–10 p.m. Tu–Th: 11:30 a.m.–11 p.m. F–
Sa: 11:30 a.m.–midnight. Brunch served Sunday.
PENN QUARTER.

More Places to See

There's so much to see and do in Washington, whether you're looking for more historic sites or browsing through the newest museums. Here is a sampling of stops you may not want to miss:

1800–1850

Chesapeake and Ohio Canal Lockkeeper's House. Stop briefly to see the only remnant of the C&O Canal Extension, the waterway that connected the Washington Canal with C&O Canal. This little house, built in the 1830s, served as the office for the Lockkeeper of the Canal, who kept records of barges passing here and collected tolls for the crossing between the two waterways. When railroads arrived, the canal quickly fell into disuse and disrepair, and the Lockkeeper's House closed until the early 1900s, when it served as head-

The Lockkeeper's House is the only remnant of the Washington Canal.

quarters for the National Park Police. Today it's a storage facility for park maintenance. Constitution Avenue and 17th Street, (202) 653-5190, www.nps.gov/choh. Not open to the public. Metro: Smithsonian. NATIONAL MALL.

Georgetown Market (now Dean & Deluca gourmet food store). The first public market in the Territory of Columbia opened on this land in 1795. Continuous expansion throughout the 1800s led the city to replace the original wood frame structure in 1865. When the market became obsolete as food stores sprang up throughout the growing city, the District preserved the building as a landmark until the 1960s—and today it serves as a neighborhood grocery with specialty foods from all over the world. 3276 M Street NW, (202) 342-2500, www.nps.gov/history/NR/travel/wash/dc18.htm. Daily 8 a.m.–9 p.m. Free. Metro: Foggy Bottom. GEORGETOWN.

1851–1900

Lillian and Albert Small Jewish Museum at Adas Israel Synagogue. This is the oldest existing synagogue in Washington, built by thirty-eight Jewish immigrant families in 1876. Today, this National Historic Shrine houses a museum that tells the story of the local Jewish community. Notably, Al Jolson sang for this congregation while his father was the rabbi here. Call at least twenty-four hours in advance for a tour. 701 3rd Street NW, (202) 789-0900, www.jhsgw.org. M, Tu, Th by appointment or 1–4, subject to staff availability. $3 suggested donation. Metro: Judiciary Square. JUDICIARY SQUARE.

National Building Museum (former Pension Building). The former home of the Pension Bureau, the first federal agency for veterans' affairs, this Italian Renaissance–style building has hosted many presidential inaugural balls in its extraordinary Great Hall. Civil engineer and U.S. Army General Montgomery Meigs designed the building as a memorial to Union soldiers, sailors, and marines in American Civil War, adding an exterior frieze—designed by sculptor Casper Bubert—that illustrates a parade of military Civil War units. Veterans could see and appreciate this tribute when they came to the Pension Bureau, making this a monument to the living as well as those who died in the war. 401 F Street NW, (202) 272-2448, www .nbm.org. M–Sa 10–5, Su 11–5; closed Thanksgiving, Christmas, and New Year's Day. Free. Metro: Judiciary Square. JUDICIARY SQUARE.

Arlington National Cemetery. In 1864, this property was part of the estate owned by the Custis family—most notably, the wife of General Robert E. Lee. When the government seized Arlington House and its surrounding 1,100 acres for nonpayment of taxes during the Civil War, Secretary of War Edwin Stanton ordered that the land be used for a national cemetery, a place to honor those who died in the Civil War and others whose lives deserved such recognition. Private William Henry Christman of the 67th Pennsylvania Infantry was the first military serviceman to be buried here on May 13, 1864. Since then, thousands of military personnel, astronauts, explorers, literary figures, and government officials have been interred in this hallowed ground. Stop at the visitor center for maps and

guidebooks to find your way to the resting places of John F. Kennedy, Chief Justice Oliver Wendell Holmes Jr., Supreme Court Justice Thurgood Marshall, and many military and political leaders. The cemetery is bordered by local routes 110 to the east and 27 to the south and west, and by U.S. 50 to the west and north. Arlington, Virginia, (702) 607-8000, www.arlingtoncemetery.org. Apr–Sep, 8–7; Oct–Mar, 8–5. Free; fees for parking. Metro: Arlington National Cemetery. ARLINGTON.

Arlington National Cemetery is a must-see for every tourist.

1901–1950

Department of the Interior Museum. Designed by architect Waddy B. Wood, the Interior's 1935 building was the first new government building construction authorized by the Franklin Roosevelt administration, and its combination of modern and classical architecture unites the concepts of economy and utility that typified this president's principles. Call ahead to schedule a tour of the building, or tour the public areas and museum on your own, and gain an understanding of the Department of the Interior's role in preserving and managing America's natural resources and most spectacular scenic wonders. The building also features a collection of Native American murals, which you can see on the guided tour. 1849 C Street NW, (202) 208-4743, www.interior.gov. M–F 8:30–4:30, third Saturday of every month 1–4; closed Sunday and federal holidays. Free. Metro: Farragut West. DOWNTOWN.

Woodrow Wilson House. Wilson was the only president who chose to live in Washington after his term in office, taking up residence in this Georgian-style house designed by architect Waddy B. Wood. Built in 1915, the house still contains the shelves Wilson ordered for his 8,000-volume library, and the elevator he had installed when he was partially paralyzed from a stroke he suffered in 1919. Wilson died in 1924 in the upstairs bedroom, but his wife, Edith Bolling Galt, lived here until 1961. You'll see the furnishings, portraits, books, photographs of world leaders, and a Gobelin tapestry that belonged to the Wilsons while they lived here. 2340 S Street NW, (202) 387-4062, www.woodrowwilsonhouse. org. T–Su 10–4. Closed Monday, Thanksgiving, Christmas, and New Year's Day. $10 adults, $8 seniors 62+, $5 students, free for children 11 and under. Metro: Dupont Circle. DUPONT CIRCLE.

Phillips Collection at Duncan Phillips House. Art collector and author Duncan Phillips opened this gallery in his home in 1921 to share his collection of paintings with the public. The collection includes works by El Greco, Manet, Renoir, Van Gogh, Monet, Degas, Gaugin, and Cezanne, representing America's first museum of modern art. 1600 21st Street NW, (202) 387-2151, www.phillipscollection .org. T–Sat 10–5, Th 10–8:30, Su 11–6. Metro: Dupont Circle. DUPONT CIRCLE.

Embassy Gulf Service Station. Constructed by Gulf Oil with materials and design associated with community mainstays like banks and libraries, this remarkable gas station was one of sixty Gulf service stations in Washington when it was built. The National Register of Historic Places notes that the permanency of this station's construction was an "important symbol of Gulf Oil's commitment to developing gas station architecture as community assets worthy of praise and preservation." Today it's a Sunoco station. 2200 P Street NW, adjacent to Rock Creek Park, (202) 659-8560, www.nps .gov/history/nr/travel/wash/dc52.htm. Open 24 hours daily. Metro: Dupont Circle. GEORGETOWN.

This gas station is on the National Register of Historic Places.

1951–2000

International Spy Museum. The only public museum in the United States dedicated to espionage, this fascinating museum displays all kinds of artifacts related to "tradecraft," the necessities for staying undercover and alive while serving the government. Stories of individual spies and the history of espionage are told in interactive and video exhibits, providing insights on the role of spying in historic and current events. 800 F Street NW, (866) 779-6873, (202) EYE-SPY-U, www.spymuseum.org. Daily 10–6, extended hours on weekends; closed New Year's Day, Thanksgiving, and Christmas. Adults $21.95, seniors 65+ and military $15.95, youths (7–11) $14.95, children 6 and under free. Metro: Gallery Place/Chinatown. PENN QUARTER.

Newseum. If you're addicted to the news, you'll love this 250,000-square-foot interactive experience, featuring seven levels of galleries and loaded with hands-on exhibits. You'll learn how news came to be and how it is disseminated to every household around the world, and you'll even have the opportunity to try your hand at accurate reporting against a deadline. Visitors often linger in the 9/11 Gallery, where they gain a better understanding of the challenges journalists faced in covering the 2001 terrorist attacks. 555 Pennsylvania Avenue NW, (202) 292-6100, www.newseum.org. Daily 9–5; closed Thanksgiving, Christmas, and New Year's Day. Adults $22.95, seniors (ages 65+) $18.95, youth 7–18 $13.95, ages 6 and under free. Metro: Archives/Navy Memorial/Penn Quarter Station. DOWNTOWN.

Glossary

abolition/abolitionists. The movement to end slavery in America. Abolitionists believed that all human beings should have equal rights, and people of one race should not have the option of owning people of other races.

Adamesque. A popular architectural style in England in the late eighteenth century, developed by Robert Adam. Adam based his new concepts on his study of excavations of the ruins at Pompeii and other ancient Greek cities, through which he discovered that the neoclassical style often departed from the rigid geometrics to emphasize decoration. He adapted the Federal style to include elements like six-pane windows, cornices with decorative molding, and an elliptical window over the front door.

Beaux-Arts style. This is a French architectural style that influenced American design during the late-nineteenth and early-twentieth centuries. Combining symmetry with opulence, this style incorporates sculpture and bas-relief into the building's form, often including garlands, gargoyles, Egyptian cartouches, projected columns (pilasters), and many other decorative forms. Interiors often feature grandly arched ceilings decorated with mosaics and murals.

Beltway. The Interstate 495 highway loop that circles the city and suburbs of Washington, DC, is often referred to as the Capital Beltway. Referring to someone as "inside the Beltway" is a way of calling him or her a political insider.

boycott. A social protest method popularized in the twentieth century, a boycott is a peaceful abstention from the use of a service or the patronage of an establishment. For example, black citizens boycotted the bus service in Montgomery, Alabama, after Rosa Parks was arrested for refusing to give up her seat to a white rider and move to the back of the bus. The bus service's resulting loss of revenue finally resulted in a change in the law, as the U.S. Supreme Court determined that segregation on buses was illegal.

civil rights movement. The effort in the United States in the 1950s and 1960s to abolish racial discrimination and segregation in the southern states. Before 1964, black citizens in some states were prevented from voting—a Constitutional right—by laws invented in these states that made unreasonable demands on African-Americans to be eligible to vote. These so-called Jim Crow laws also segregated public facilities, restaurants, and even drinking fountains, while creating "separate but equal" public schools for black children. Through a movement of peaceful resistance, led by Dr. Martin Luther King Jr., African-Americans used nonviolent methods to protest their treatment until President Lyndon Johnson abolished segregation with the Civil Rights Act of 1964.

Georgian style. A wide range of architectural styles that were popular between 1720 and 1840, named for Kings George I, II, III, and IV of England who reigned during this time period. The symmetrical Palladian style, ornate Gothic architecture, and the Roman-inspired neoclassical design are all considered parts of the Georgian era.

Gothic architecture. Also known as "the French style," Gothic architecture became especially popular in medieval times from the late twelfth century into the sixteenth century. Many of Europe's most impressive cathedrals and castles feature these strikingly detailed design elements. Buildings constructed in the Gothic style in the nineteenth century are considered Gothic Revival.

integration. Before 1964, it was legal in some states to separate white people from people of color in restaurants, public facilities, and schools. The Civil Rights Act of 1964 integrated all pubic facilities and services, making it illegal to refuse service to any person based on the color of his or her skin.

melting pot. As people from every country in the world arrived in the United States—especially in the late 1800s and early 1900s—politicians and historians referred to the blending of cultures, languages, and ideas as a "melting pot," bringing all of these disparate elements together to create a unified America.

mosaic. An art form in which the artist creates a picture, scene, or abstract using pieces of colored glass, china, ceramic tile, stone, or other colorful materials. Such works of art were particularly popular in Beaux-Arts or Gothic churches and public buildings in the nineteenth century.

Reconstruction. When the American Civil War ended in 1865, many southern states were in shambles: Battle and occupation led to the destruction of homes, cities, cropland, and transportation, making it impossible for the former

Confederate states to rebuild on their own. The United States put a program in place to reconstruct the infrastructure in the southern states, gaining federal control of each state and ensuring that the black slaves had been freed before providing materials, funds, and assistance in rebuilding Southern society. Reconstruction reached its conclusion in 1877.

Romanesque style. An architectural style descended from Roman design, predating Gothic construction in the Middle Ages by several hundred years. Thick walls, massive archways, high towers, and ornamental elements are all part of this style, stopping short of the elaborate decoration that typified the Gothic style.

segregation. For 101 years from the abolition of slavery in 1863, it was legal in some states to separate black citizens from white in public facilities, schools, churches, and even rest rooms. Signs that said WHITES ONLY and COLOREDS ONLY were commonplace, and there were stiff penalties for disobedience, ranging from public humiliation to police brutality and jail time. The civil rights movement of the 1950s and 1960s used peaceful resistance to bring the absurdity of such laws to the nation's attention, resulting in passage of the Civil Rights Act of 1964 and the integration of schools and public buildings.

sortie. The deployment of a single military unit—a ship, a plane, or (as in the Civil War) a regiment or brigade.

Bibliography and Suggested Reading

Bordewich, Fergus. *Washington: The Making of the American Capital.* New York: Amistad (Harper-Collins), 2008.

"Boundary Stones of the District of Columbia," www.boundarystones.org.

Carrier, Thomas J. *Washington, DC: A Historical Walking Tour.* Charleston, SC: Arcadia Publishing, 2005.

Gilmore, Matthew. "A Timeline of Washington DC History." H-Net: Humanities and Social Sciences Online. www.h-net.org/~dclist/timeline1.html

Gutheim, Frederick. *Worthy of the Nation: Washington, DC, from L'Enfant to the National Capital Planning Commission.* Baltimore: The Johns Hopkins University Press, 2006.

Heritage Preservation Services, American Battlefield Protection Program. "Fort Stevens," *Civil War Sites Advisory Commission Battle Summaries,* www.nps.gov/hps/abpp/battles/dc001.htm.

The Historical Society of Washington, DC "DC History Resources," www.historydc.org/resources/.

Minetor, Randi S. *Passport To Your National Parks Companion Guide: National Capital Region.* Guilford, Conn.: The Globe Pequot Press, 2008.

Mitchell, Alexander D. *Washington, DC, Then and Now.* San Diego, Calif.: Thunder Bay Press, 1999.

National Park Service Web site, www.nps.gov.

National Register of Historic Places website, www. nps.gov/nr.

Solomon, Mary Jane, Barbara Ruben, and Rebecca Aloisi. *Insider's Guide: Washington, DC* Guilford, Conn.: The Globe Pequot Press, 2007.

Standiford, Les. *Washington Burning: How a Frenchman's Vision for Our Nation's Capital Survived Congress, the Founding Fathers, and the Invading British Army.* New York: Crown Publishing Group, 2008.

Washington, DC

Index

Index

113

Index

Index